Mediterranean Diet Cookbook For Beginners

A 12-Weeks Smart Meal Plan With Quick and Delicious Recipes To Lose Weight And Stay Fit Easily Without Ever Giving Up The Taste of Great Food

CHRISTINA G. MORALES

© Copyright 2021 by Christina G. Morales - All rights reserved.

This document is geared towards providing exact and reliable information in regard to the topic and issue covered.

- From a Declaration of Principles which was accepted and approved equally by a Committee of the American Bar Association and a Committee of Publishers and Associations.

In no way is it legal to reproduce, duplicate, or transmit any part of this document in either electronic means or in printed format. All rights reserved.

The information provided herein is stated to be truthful and consistent, in that any liability, in terms of inattention or otherwise, by any usage or abuse of any policies, processes, or directions contained within is the solitary and utter responsibility of the recipient reader. Under no circumstances will any legal responsibility or blame be held against the publisher for any reparation, damages, or monetary loss due to the information herein, either directly or indirectly.

Respective authors own all copyrights not held by the publisher.

The information herein is offered for informational purposes solely and is universal as so. The presentation of the information is without contract or any type of guarantee assurance.

The trademarks that are used are without any consent, and the publication of the trademark is without permission or backing by the trademark owner. All trademarks and brands within this book are for clarifying purposes only and are owned by the owners themselves, not affiliated with this document.

INTRODUCTION 9
CHAPTER 1. WHAT IS THE MEDITERRANEAN DIET AND ITS ORIGINS 10
Origin of the diet 11
Mediterranean diet and other famous diets 12
CHAPTER 2. BREAKFAST 13
1. SECRET BREAKFAST SUNDAES 13
2. GREEK YOGURT PANCAKES 13
3. GREEK YOGURT W/BERRIES & SEEDS 14
4. MEDITERRANEAN BREAKFAST EGG WHITE SANDWICH 15
5. BREAKFAST TACO SCRAMBLE 15
6. BLUEBERRY GREEK YOGURT PANCAKES 16
7. CAULIFLOWER FRITTERS WITH HUMMUS 16
8. OVERNIGHT BERRY CHIA OATS 17
9. FETA AND QUINOA EGG MUFFINS 18
10. 5-MINUTE HEIRLOOM TOMATO AND CUCUMBER TOAST 18
11. GARLIC PARMESAN CHICKEN WINGS 19
12. GREEK YOGURT WITH WALNUTS AND HONEY 19
13. TAHINI PINE NUTS TOAST 19
14. FETA AVOCADO AND MASHED CHICKPEA TOAST 20
15. FETA FRITTATA 20
16. PILAF WITH CREAM CHEESE 21
17. EASY SPAGHETTI SQUASH 21
18. ROASTED EGGPLANT SALAD 22
19. SMOKED SALMON AND POACHED EGGS ON TOAST 22
20. HONEY ALMOND RICOTTA SPREAD WITH PEACHES 23
21. MEDITERRANEAN EGGS CUPS 23
22. LOW-CARB BAKED EGGS WITH AVOCADO AND FETA 24
23. MEDITERRANEAN EGGS WHITE BREAKFAST SANDWICH WITH ROASTED TOMATOES 24
24. MEDITERRANEAN FETA AND QUINOA EGG MUFFINS 25
25. BACON AND BRIE OMELET WEDGES 25
26. PASTRY-LESS SPANAKOPITA 26
27. DATE AND WALNUT OVERNIGHT OATS 26
28. PEAR AND MANGO SMOOTHIE 27
29. EGGPLANT SALAD 27
30. ARTICHOKE FRITTATA 27
31. ORANGE FISH MEAL 28
32. SHRIMP ZOODLES 28
33. ASPARAGUS TROUT MEAL 29
34. MEDITERRANEAN LENTIL SLOPPY JOES 29
35. GORGONZOLA SWEET POTATO BURGERS 30
36. ZUCCHINI-EGGPLANT GRATIN 30
37. CHICKEN GYROS WITH TZATZIKI SAUCE 31
38. CRISPY PESTO CHICKEN 32
39. BEEF STEW WITH BEANS AND ZUCCHINI 33

40. Tomato Salad 34

CHAPTER 3. LUNCH 35

41. Beef Kofta 35
42. Herb Roasted Lamb Chops 35
43. Grilled Salmon with Lemon and Wine 36
44. Beer-batter Fish 36
45. Sole with Spinach 37
46. Pickled Apple 38
47. Baked Clams Oreganata 38
48. Tuna Tartare 39
49. Cod Cakes 39
50. Grilled Vegetable Kebabs 39
51. Manchego Crackers 40
52. Burrata Caprese Stack 40
53. Zucchini-Ricotta Fritters with Lemon-Garlic Aioli 41
54. Salmon-Stuffed Cucumbers 41
55. Goat Cheese–Mackerel Pâté 42
56. White Bean Dip with Garlic and Herbs 42
57. Black Bean Dip 43
58. Salsa Verde 43
59. Greek Eggplant Dip 44
60. Baba Ghanoush 44
61. Cheesy Caprese Salad Skewers 44
62. Leafy Lacinato Tuscan Treat 45
63. Greek Guacamole Hybrid Hummus 45
64. Packed Picnic 45
65. Pizza & Pastry 46
66. Cashews and Red Cabbage Salad 47
67. Apples and Pomegranate Salad 47
68. Cranberry Bulgur Mix 47
69. Chickpeas, Corn and Black Beans Salad 48
70. Olives and Lentils Salad 48
71. Lime Spinach and Chickpeas Salad 48
72. Minty Olives and Tomatoes Salad 48
73. Roasted Beet Salad with Ricotta Cheese 49
74. Baked Fish with Tomatoes and Mushrooms 49
75. Goat Cheese and Walnut Salad 50
76. Grilled Spiced Turkey Burger 50
77. Tomato Tea Party Sandwiches 51
78. Veggie Shish Kebabs 51
79. Crispy Falafel 52
80. Onion Fried Eggs 52

CHAPTER 4. DINNER 54

81. Savoy Cabbage with Coconut Cream Sauce 54
82. Slow Cooked Buttery Mushrooms 54
83. Steamed Squash Chowder 54

84.	Steamed Zucchini-Paprika	55
85.	Stir Fried Brussels sprouts and Carrots	55
86.	Stir Fried Eggplant	56
87.	Summer Vegetables	56
88.	Stir Fried Bok Choy	57
89.	Summer Veggies in Instant Pot	57
90.	Sumptuous Tomato Soup	58
91.	Avocado Peach Salsa on Grilled Swordfish	58
92.	Breaded and Spiced Halibut	59
93.	Berries and Grilled Calamari	59
94.	Coconut Salsa on Chipotle Fish Tacos	60
95.	Baked Cod Crusted with Herbs	61
96.	Cajun Garlic Shrimp Noodle Bowl	61
97.	Crazy Saganaki Shrimp	62
98.	Creamy Bacon-Fish Chowder	62
99.	Crisped Coco-Shrimp with Mango Dip	63
100.	Cucumber-Basil Salsa on Halibut Pouches	63
101.	Chicken Zucchini Boats	64
102.	Urban Chicken Alfredo	64
103.	Grilled Chicken and Zucchini Kebabs	65
104.	Gyro Burgers with Tahini Sauce	66
105.	Baked Parmesan Chicken Wraps	66
106.	Greek Flavor Tomato Chicken Pasta	67
107.	Spinach and Feta–Stuffed Chicken Breasts	67
108.	Mango Chicken Salad	68
109.	Tender Chicken Quesadilla	68
110.	Chicken Bolognese	69
111.	Jerk Chicken	69
112.	Pomegranate Chicken Thighs	70
113.	Butter Chicken	70
114.	Mediterranean Pearl Couscous	71
115.	Potato and Tuna Salad	71
116.	Tuna with Vegetable Mix	72
117.	Tuna Bowl with Kale	72
118.	Greek Baked Cod	73
119.	Poultry and Meat 2 Tender Lamb Chops	74
120.	Seasoned Pork Chops	74

CHAPTER 5. SNACKS 75

121.	Chocolate Matcha Balls	75
122.	Chia Almond Butter Pudding	75
123.	Refreshing Strawberry Popsicles	75
124.	Dark Chocolate Mousse	76
125.	Warm & Soft Baked Pears	76
126.	Healthy & Quick Energy Bites	76
127.	Creamy Yogurt Banana Bowls	77
128.	Chicken Wings Platter	77
129.	Carrot Spread	77

130.	Chocolate Mousse	78
131.	Veggie Fritters	78
132.	White Bean Dip	79
133.	Eggplant Dip	79
134.	Bulgur Lamb Meatballs	79
135.	Roasted Parmesan Broccoli	80
136.	Cucumber Hummus Sandwiches	80
137.	Banana Strawberry Popsicles	81
138.	Cajun Walnuts and Olives Bowls	81
139.	Mango Salsa	81
140.	Blackberries Caprese Skewers	82
141.	Yogurt Dip	82
142.	Tomato Bruschetta	82
143.	Pepper Tapenade	83
144.	Red Pepper Hummus	83
145.	Cucumber Bites	83
146.	Stuffed Avocado	84
147.	Hummus with Ground Lamb	84
148.	Wrapped Plums	84
149.	Cucumber Sandwich Bites	85
150.	Cucumber Rolls	85
151.	Olives and Cheese Stuffed Tomatoes	85
152.	Tomato Salsa	86
153.	Chili Mango and Watermelon Salsa	86
154.	Creamy Spinach and Shallots Dip	86
155.	Feta Artichoke Dip	87
156.	Avocado Dip	87
157.	Goat Cheese and Chives Spread	87
158.	Stuffed Chicken	88
159.	Cinnamon Baby Back Ribs Platter	88
160.	Buttery Carrot Sticks	88

CHAPTER 6. DESERTS 90

161.	Maple Vanilla Baked Pears	90
162.	Easy roasted fruit recipe	90
163.	Triple Chocolate Tiramisu	91
164.	Easy Strawberry Crepes Recipe	92
165.	Dried Fruit Compote	92
166.	Chocolate Rice Pudding	93
167.	Fruit Compote	93
168.	Stuffed Apples	94
169.	Cinnamon-Stewed Dried Plums with Greek Yogurt	94
170.	Vanilla-Poached Apricots	95
171.	Creamy Spiced Almond Milk	95
172.	Poached Pears with Greek Yogurt and Pistachio	95
173.	Peaches Poached in Rose Water	96
174.	Brown Betty Apple Dessert	96
175.	Blueberry Oat Crumble	97

- 176. Date and Walnut Cookies 98
- 177. Moroccan Stuffed Dates 98
- 178. Fig Cookies 98
- 179. Turkish delight Cookies 99
- 180. Anise Cookies 99
- 181. Spanish Nougat 100
- 182. Spanish Crumble Cakes 100
- 183. Greek Honey Cookies 101
- 184. Cinnamon Butter Cookies 101
- 185. Best French Meringues 102
- 186. Cinnamon Palmier 102
- 187. Honey Sesame Cookies 103
- 188. Baked Apples 103
- 189. Pumpkin Baked with Dry Fruit 104
- 190. Banana Shake Bowls 104
- 191. Cold Lemon Squares 104
- 192. Blackberry and Apples Cobbler 104
- 193. Black Tea Cake 105
- 194. Green Tea and Vanilla Cream 105
- 195. Vermicelli Pudding 106
- 196. Strawberry Compote in Red Wine Syrup 106
- 197. Homemade Caramel-Dipped Apples 106
- 198. Pomegranate-Pistachio Bark 107
- 199. Coconut-Date Pudding 107
- 200. Honey Almonds 108

CHAPTER 7. SHOPPING LIST 109

- *Non-starchy vegetables (maximum 2-3 servings per day)* 109
- *Fruits (maximum 2-3 servings per day)* 109
- *Grains (maximum 7 servings per week)* 109
- *Starchy vegetables (maximum 3 servings per week)* 109
- *Grains including bread (maximum 7 servings per week)* 109
- *Dairy (maximum 3 servings per day)* 109
- *Vegetable oils (maximum 7 servings per week)* 110
- *Nuts (maximum 7 servings per week)* 110
- *Beans (maximum 7 servings per week)* 110
- *Dried fruit (maximum 1 serving per day)* 110

CHAPTER 8. 10 TIPS FOR SUCCESS 111

- *Treat Yourself like A Guest* 111
- *Learn to Savor* 111
- *Become a Social Eater* 111
- *Learn to Make Substitutions* 111
- *Get Some Moderate Exercise Every Day—Preferably Outdoors* 111
- *Don't Tempt Yourself* 112
- *Don't Overwhelm Yourself* 112
- *Give Yourself a Break* 112
- *Try Something New Each Week* 112

Try Growing Your Own *112*

CHAPTER 9. 12-WEEK MEAL PROGRAM **113**
    WEEK 1 113
    WEEK 2 114
    WEEK 3 115
    WEEK 4 116
    WEEK 5 117
    WEEK 6 118
    WEEK 7 119
    WEEK 8 120
    WEEK 9 121
    WEEK 10 122
    WEEK 11 123
    WEEK 12 124

CONCLUSION **125**

INTRODUCTION

It's not about the food, it's about the life style.

Diet is often on the mind of many people. There are so many diets floating around today that it can be difficult to find a diet that delivers real results. One diet that has been gaining popularity lately is centered around a Mediterranean lifestyle: better known these days as "The Mediterranean Diet." That diet is rich in veggies, fruits, whole grains, beans and legumes, nuts and seeds, olive oil and red wine.

These foods are most often high in monounsaturated fat.

This diet emphasizes the consumption of vegetables, fruits, grains, legumes, and nuts in moderation while avoiding saturated fat-laden foods.

The Mediterranean diet can also help you lose weight by reducing your overall calorie intake because the foods in a Mediterranean diet are very filling and satiating. Also, if you're used to eating a lot of red meat, dairy products, and refined grains, trying to exchange these items for their healthier Mediterranean counterparts won't leave you feeling deprived.

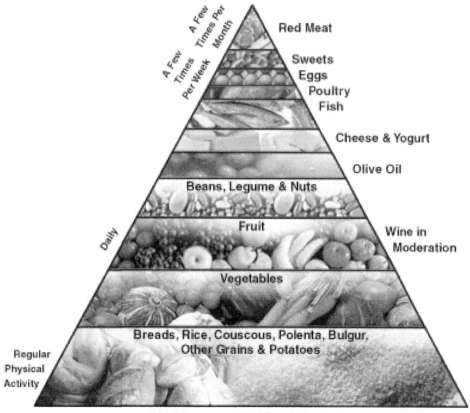

Mediterranean Diet Food Pyramid

CHAPTER 1. WHAT IS THE MEDITERRANEAN DIET AND ITS ORIGINS

The Mediterranean diet is a food pattern characterized by vegetables, fruit, whole grains, nuts, legumes (beans), olive oil and low-fat dairy products. The traditional med diet – which was once considered a dietary prescription for health – is high in unsaturated fat with a limited intake of saturated fat. In addition to these nutritional characteristics, Mediterranean cuisine traditionally favors fresh fruits and vegetables served by themselves rather than as ingredients in dishes that rely heavily on meat or dairy products.

Mediterranean diet is an umbrella term used to describe a way of eating that is common in countries that border the Mediterranean Sea.

Mediterranean diet typically includes four to five daily meals or snacks.

Mediterranean diet is high in carbohydrate foods with a lower amount of fat and lower amount of meat and protein.

It is high in fiber from fruits and vegetables. Most of the carbs are coming from vegetables. It is higher in whole grains than in other North European diets with a lower amount of refined grains.

It is high in olive oil (more than most Western countries).

It has lower intakes of sodium, saturated fat and cholesterol than most other countries with the Western diet. The Mediterranean diet has some animal fats including low-fat dairy products and less red meat compared to other countries with the Western diet.

Origin of the diet

What first needs mentioning is that there's no strict definition for what constitutes a "Mediterranean Diet." In general terms, it usually includes lots of fruits and vegetables, oils from olives or canola oil, moderate amounts of seafood such as cod or tuna with low mercury levels (due to pollution), and goat yogurt. Of course, the Mediterranean diet is a lot more than this basic description. It includes many cultures and these cultures have their own unique diet. The reason for this is that the Mediterranean region has always been far more diverse than other parts of the world (more on this later).

Therefore, it's difficult to speak about the origins of the Mediterranean Diet as a whole but many scholars agree that there are commonalities between several communities within the region. Martin Baumgarten, a historian who studied over 400 cultures and looked at dietary patterns, did find similarities in several cultures; however, he would often point out differences between them as well. He would focus on different dietary patterns of the cultures that he studied (such as the Slavic culture) and note how they differed from each other.

One of these differences is between traditional Mediterranean diets (that consisted of wild-farmed olives and seafood) and the modernized Mediterranean diets (which include more processed foods). Baumgarten argues that these shifts likely occurred because different cultural groups wanted to court followers within their community, not necessarily for reasons of health. He says that "the link between culture and eating habits is so strong that it can change over time; it's not a genetic issue.

One thing that can be said about the Mediterranean diet is that it's always existed, at least in some form. Not only that but some people speculate the diet has been around for over 6,000 years, a full millennium before the first civilizations of Mesopotamia and Egypt arose.

Mediterranean diet and other famous diets

The Mediterranean Diet is considered healthier than other famous diets like the Atkins diet or the Paleo diet because it includes a high intake of plant-based foods and has a healthy balance of fats.
The Mediterranean diet was originally a diet consumed in the nine countries around the Mediterranean sea. However, nowadays it has been adapted to be more inclusive of different cultures and foods as well as more geographically broader.
The Mediterranean diet consists of:
- High consumption of fruits and vegetables
- High consumption of nuts, seeds legumes and beans
- Moderate consumption of fish (particularly omega-3 rich)
- Moderate consumption of poultry, eggs & dairy products
- Low intake of red meat & processed meat
- No or very little sugar

How is it different to other diets?

The key difference between the Mediterranean diet and other diets is that it excludes dairy products. This is especially important as 1) dairy has been shown to increase insulin resistance and 2) it promotes inflammation.
This makes the Mediterranean diet a lot more beneficial for those who are lactose intolerant and who suffer from adverse gastrointestinal effects from consuming dairy products.
Furthermore, if you're trying to lose weight while retaining your muscle mass, then the fact that a high intake of protein can promote both muscle gain and fat loss means that having a low protein intake (which is common in Mediterranean diets) will help you preserve your lean body mass while losing fat.
Finally, the fats consumed in the Mediterranean diet are also very important as they are primarily unsaturated fats.
In other words, the Mediterranean diet is a healthy way of living for those who want to stay healthy and maintain good cardiovascular health.

CHAPTER 2. BREAKFAST

1. Secret Breakfast Sundaes

Level of difficulty: Novice level
Preparation Time: 5 minutes
Cooking Time: 12 minutes
Servings: 4
Ingredients:

- 6 Slices of Bacon
- 1/2 cup of Heavy Whipping Cream
- 5 tbsp. of Pure Maple Syrup or Pancake Syrup 3 tbsp. of Light Brown Sugar
- 3/4 cup of Granola Cereal 2 cups of Coffee Ice Cream
- 2 cups of Butter Pecan Ice Cream
- 4 Fresh Strawberries

Directions:
1. Preheat your oven to 400 degrees. Arrange your bacon on a non-stick baking sheet. Sprinkle 1/2 of your brown sugar over the bacon—Bake for approximately 6 minutes. Turn the bacon and sprinkle the remaining brown sugar over it. Bake for an additional 6 minutes until bacon is dark brown. Remove from your oven and allow cooling on a wire rack. Once your bacon has cooled, crumble it up and set it aside.
2. Beat together with a tbsp., maple syrup with a 1/2 cup of Heavy Whipping cream in a 2-quart metal bowl using an electric mixer. Spoon 2 tbsp. of granola into four parfait glasses. Evenly scoop the butter pecan ice cream into glasses and sprinkle them with your remaining granola. Add your coffee ice cream to each glass and evenly drizzle the remaining maple syrup on top. Sprinkle with your bacon and top with strawberries.
3. Serve and Enjoy!

Nutrition:
- Calories: 329 kcal
- Protein: 7.42 g
- Fat: 27.55 g
- Carbohydrates: 14.41 g

2. Greek Yogurt Pancakes

Level of difficulty: Novice level
Preparation Time: 20 minutes
Cooking Time: 5 minutes
Servings: 4
Ingredients:

- A cup of Old-Fashioned Oats
- 2 tbsp. of Flax Seeds

- 1 tsp. of Baking Soda
- 1/2 cup of All-Purpose Flour
- 1/4 tsp. of Salt
- 2 cups of Vanilla Greek Yogurt
- 2 tbsp. of Honey or Agave 2 Large Eggs
- 2 tbsp. of Canola Oil Syrup

Directions:
1. Combine oats, seeds, flour, baking soda, and salt in your blender and pulse for approximately 30 seconds.
2. Add in your eggs, yogurt, agave, and oil. Blend until it is smooth. Let your batter stand for approximately 20 minutes to thicken.
3. Heat your skillet over medium heat. Brush your skillet with oil. Spoon your batter 1/4 of a cup at a time into your skillet. Cook your pancakes until the bottoms turn golden brown, and bubbles begin forming on top. It should take about 2 minutes. Turn over your pancakes and cook until the bottoms are golden brown. It should take another 2 minutes.
4. Transfer pancakes to your baking sheet. Keep warm in your oven. Repeat the process until all your batter is cooked.
5. Add on desired syrup and fruit toppings.

Serve and Enjoy!

Nutrition:
- Calories: 172 kcal
- Protein: 6.62 g
- Fat: 4.06 g
- Carbohydrates: 37.01 g

3. Greek Yogurt w/Berries & Seeds

Level of difficulty: Novice level
Preparation Time: 3 minutes
Cooking Time: 0 minutes
Servings: 1
Ingredients:
- One handful of Blueberries
- One handful of Raspberries
- 1 tbsp. of Greek Yogurt
- 1 tsp. of Sunflower Seeds
- 1 tsp. of Pumpkin Seeds
- 1 tsp. of Sliced Almonds

Directions:
1. Wash and dry your berries. Place them into a dish.
2. Spoon your Greek yogurt on top and sprinkle it with your seeds and Almonds.
3. Serve and Enjoy!

Nutrition:
- Calories: 127 kcal
- Protein: 2.28 g
- Fat: 3.66 g
- Carbohydrates: 23.49 g

4. Mediterranean Breakfast Egg White Sandwich

Level of difficulty: Novice level
Preparation Time: 15 minutes.
Cooking Time: 30 minutes.
Servings: 1
Ingredients:
- 1 tsp. vegan butter.
- ¼ cup egg whites.
- 1 tsp. chopped fresh herbs such as parsley, basil, rosemary.
- 1 whole-grain seeded ciabatta roll.
- 1 tbsp. pesto.
- 1 or 2 slices Muenster cheese (or other cheese such as provolone, Monterey jack, etc.)
- About ½ cup roasted tomatoes.
- Salt, to taste.
- Pepper, to taste.

For the roasted tomatoes:
- 10 oz. grape tomatoes.
- 1 tbsp. extra virgin olive oil.
- Kosher salt, to taste.
- Coarse black pepper, to taste.

Directions:
1. In a small nonstick skillet over medium heat, melt the vegan butter. Pour in egg whites, season with salt and pepper, sprinkle with fresh herbs, cook for 3 to 4 minutes or until egg is done, flip once.
2. In the meantime, toast the ciabatta bread in the toaster. Once done, spread both halves with pesto.
3. Place the egg on the bottom half of the sandwich roll, folding if necessary, top with cheese, add the roasted tomatoes and top half of the rolled sandwich.
4. For the roasted tomatoes, preheat the oven to 400° F. Slice tomatoes in half lengthwise. Then place them onto a baking sheet and drizzle with the olive oil, toss to coat.
5. Season with salt and pepper and roast in the oven for about 20 minutes, until the skin appears wrinkled

Nutrition:
- Calories: 458.
- Carbs: 51 g.
- Fat: 0 g.
- Protein: 21 g.

5. Breakfast Taco Scramble

Level of difficulty: Novice level
Preparation Time: 15 minutes.
Cooking Time: 1 hour and 25 minutes.
Servings: 4
Ingredients:
- 8 large eggs, beaten.
- ¼ tsp. seasoning salt.
- 1 lb. 99% lean ground turkey.
- 2 tbsp. Greek seasoning.
- ½ small onion, minced.
- 2 tbsp. bell pepper, minced.
- 4 oz. can tomato sauce.
- ¼ cup water.

For the potatoes:
- 12 (1 lb.) baby gold or red potatoes, quartered.
- 4 tsp. olive oil.
- ¾ Tsp. salt.
- ½ tsp. garlic powder.
- Fresh black pepper, to taste.

Directions:
1. In a large bowl, beat the eggs, season with seasoning salt. Preheat the oven to 425° F. Spray a 9x12 or large oval casserole dish with cooking oil.
2. Add the potatoes, 1 tbsp. oil, ¾ tsp. salt, garlic powder and black pepper

and toss to coat. Bake for 45 minutes to 1 hour, tossing every 15 minutes.
3. In the meantime, brown the turkey in a large skillet over medium heat, breaking it up while it cooks. Once no longer pink, add in the Greek seasoning.
4. Add in the bell pepper, onion, tomato sauce and water, stir and cover, simmer on low for about 20 minutes. Spray a different skillet with nonstick spray over medium heat.
5. Once heated, add in the eggs seasoned with ¼ tsp. salt and scramble for 2 to 3 minutes, or cook until it sets.
6. Distribute 3/4 cup turkey and 2/3 cup eggs and divide the potatoes in each storage container, store for 3 to 4 days.

Nutrition:
- Calories: 450.
- Fat: 19 g.
- Carbs: 24.5 g.
- Protein: 46 g.

6. Blueberry Greek Yogurt Pancakes

Level of difficulty: Novice level
Preparation Time: 15 minutes.
Cooking Time: 15 minutes.
Servings: 6
Ingredients:
- 1 ¼ cup all-purpose flour.
- 2 tsp. baking powder.
- 1 tsp. baking soda.
- ¼ tsp. salt.
- ¼ cup sugar.
- 3 eggs.
- 3 tbsp. vegan butter unsalted, melted.
- ½ cup milk.
- 1 ½ cups Greek yogurt plain, non-fat.
- ½ cup blueberries optional.

Toppings:
- Greek yogurt.
- Mixed berries (blueberries, raspberries and blackberries).

Directions:
1. In a large bowl, whisk together the flour, salt, baking powder and baking soda. In a separate bowl, whisk together butter, sugar, eggs, Greek yogurt, and milk until the mixture is smooth.
2. Then add in the Greek yogurt mixture from step to the dry mixture in step 1, mix to combine, allow the batter to sit for 20 minutes to get a smooth texture. If using blueberries fold them into the pancake batter.
3. Heat the pancake griddle, spray with non-stick butter spray or just brush with butter. Pour the batter, in ¼ cupful's, onto the griddle.
4. Cook until the bubbles on top burst and create small holes, lift up the corners of the pancake to see if they're golden brown on the bottom
5. With a wide spatula, flip the pancake and cook on the other side until lightly browned. Serve.

Nutrition:
- Calories: 258.
- Carbs: 33 g.
- Fat: 8 g.
- Protein: 11 g.

7. Cauliflower Fritters with Hummus

Level of difficulty: Novice level
Preparation Time: 15 minutes.
Cooking Time: 15 minutes.
Servings: 4
Ingredients:
- 2 (15 oz.) cans chickpeas, divided.

- 2 ½ tbsp. olive oil, divided, plus more for frying.
- 1 cup onion, chopped, about ½ a small onion.
- 2 tbsp. garlic, minced.
- 2 cups cauliflower, cut into small pieces, about ½ a large head.
- ½ tsp. salt.
- Black pepper.

Topping:
- Hummus, of choice.
- Green onion, diced.

Directions:
1. Preheat oven to 400° F. Rinse and drain 1 can of the chickpeas, place them on a paper towel to dry off well.
2. Then place the chickpeas into a large bowl, removing the loose skins that come off, and toss with 1 tbsp. olive oil. Spread the chickpeas onto a large pan and sprinkle with salt and pepper.
3. Bake for 20 minutes, then stir and then bake an additional 5 to 10 minutes until very crispy.
4. Once the chickpeas are roasted, transfer them to a large food processor and process them until broken down and crumble. Don't over process them and turn them into flour, as you need to have some texture. Place the mixture into a small bowl, set aside.
5. In a large pan over medium-high heat, add the remaining 1 ½ tbsp. olive oil. Once heated, add in the onion and garlic, cook until lightly golden brown, about 2 minutes.
6. Then add in the chopped cauliflower, cook for an additional 2 minutes, until the cauliflower is golden.
7. Turn the heat down to low and cover the pan, cook until the cauliflower is fork-tender and the onions are golden brown and caramelized, stirring often about 3 to 5 minutes.
8. Transfer the cauliflower mixture to the food processor, drain and rinse the remaining can of chickpeas and add them into the food processor, along with the salt and a pinch of pepper.
9. Blend until smooth, and the mixture starts to ball, stop to scrape down the sides as needed
10. Transfer the cauliflower mixture into a large bowl and add in ¼ cup of the roasted chickpea crumbs, stir until well combined.
11. In a large bowl over medium heat, add in enough oil to lightly cover the bottom of a large pan. Working in batches, cook the patties until golden brown, about 2 to 3 minutes, flip and cook again. Serve.

Nutrition:
- Calories: 333.
- Carbs: 45 g.
- Fat: 13 g.
- Protein: 14 g.

8. Overnight Berry Chia Oats

Level of difficulty: Novice level
Preparation Time: 15 minutes.
Cooking Time: 5 minutes.
Servings: 1
Ingredients:
- ½ cup Quaker oats rolled oats.
- ¼ cup chia seeds.
- 1 cup milk or water.
- Pinch of salt and cinnamon
- Maple syrup, or a different sweetener, to taste.
- 1 cup frozen berries of choice or smoothie leftovers.

Toppings:
- Yogurt

- Berries

Directions:
1. In a jar with a lid, add the oats, seeds, milk, salt and cinnamon and refrigerate overnight. On serving day, puree the berries in a blender.
2. Stir the oats, add in the berry puree and top with yogurt and more berries, nuts, honey, or garnish of your choice. Enjoy!

Nutrition:
- Calories: 405.
- Carbs: 65 g.
- Fat: 11 g.
- Protein: 17 g.

9. Feta and Quinoa Egg Muffins

Level of difficulty: Intermediate
Preparation Time: 20 minutes.
Cooking Time: 45 to 50 minutes.
Servings: 12
Ingredients:
- 1 cup cooked quinoa.
- 2 cups baby spinach, chopped.
- ½ cup kalamata olives.
- 1 cup tomatoes.
- ½ cup white onion.
- 1 tbsp. fresh oregano.
- ½ tsp. salt.
- 2 tsp. + more for coating pans olive oil.
- 8 eggs.
- 1 cup crumbled feta cheese.
- 12-cup muffin tin.

Directions:
1. Heat the oven to reach 350° F. Lightly grease the muffin tray cups with a spritz of cooking oil.
2. Prepare a skillet using the medium temperature setting and add the oil. When it's hot, toss in the onions to sauté for 2 minutes.
3. Dump the tomatoes into the skillet and sauté for one minute. Fold in the spinach and continue cooking until the leaves have wilted (1 min.).
4. Transfer the pot to the countertop and add the oregano and olives. Set it aside.
5. Crack the eggs into a mixing bowl, using an immersion stick blender to mix them thoroughly. Add the cooked veggies in with the rest of the fixings.
6. Stir until it's combined and scoop the mixture into the greased muffin cups. Set the timer to bake the muffins for 30 minutes until browned, and the muffins are set. Cool for about ten minutes. Serve.

Nutrition:
- Calories: 295.
- Carbs: 3 g.
- Fat: 23 g.
- Protein: 19 g.

10. 5-Minute Heirloom Tomato and Cucumber Toast

Level of difficulty: Novice level
Preparation Time: 10 minutes.
Cooking Time: 6 to 10 minutes.
Servings: 1
Ingredients:
- 1 small heirloom tomato.
- 1 Persian cucumber.
- 1 tsp. olive oil.
- 1 pinch oregano.
- Kosher salt and pepper as desired.
- 2 tsp. low-fat whipped cream cheese.
- 2 pieces trader Joe's whole grain crispbread or your choice.
- 1 tsp. balsamic glaze.

Directions:
1. Dice the cucumber and tomato.

2. Combine all the fixings except for the cream cheese.
3. Smear the cheese on the bread and add the mixture. Top it off with the balsamic glaze and serve.

Nutrition:
- Calories: 239.
- Carbs: 32 g.
- Fat: 11 g.
- Protein: 7 g.

11. Garlic Parmesan Chicken Wings

Level of difficulty: Novice level
Preparation Time: 10 minutes.
Cooking Time: 35 minutes.
Servings: 4
Ingredients:
- 16 chicken wings, pasture-raised.
- 2 tsp. minced garlic.
- 2 tsp. minced parsley.
- ¼ cup olive oil.
- ¼ cup unsalted butter.
- 1 cup grated parmesan cheese, full-fat.
- 2 tbsp. chopped basil leaves.

Directions:
1. Set oven to 450° F and let preheat.
2. In the meantime, place a large skillet pan over medium-high heat, add oil and when hot, add chicken wings.
3. Cook for 3 minutes per side until seared and then transfer pan to heated oven.
4. Bake chicken wings for 20 to 30 minutes or until nicely golden brown and crispy.
5. When done, return pan over medium heat, add garlic and butter and cook until butter melt completely and chicken is well coated with the butter-garlic mixture.
6. Sprinkle cheese over chicken wings and remove the pan from heat.
7. Garnish with basil and serve.

Nutrition:
- Calories: 259.
- Carbs: 1.2 g.
- Fat: 20.3 g.
- Protein: 17.5 g.
- Fiber: 0.1 g.

12. Greek Yogurt with Walnuts and Honey

Level of difficulty: Novice level
Preparation Time: 5 minutes.
Cooking Time: 0 minutes.
Servings: 4
Ingredients:
- 4 cups Greek yogurt, fat-free, plain or vanilla.
- ½ cup California walnuts, toasted, chopped.
- 3 tbsp. honey or agave nectar.
- Fresh fruit, chopped or granola, low-fat (both optional).

Directions:
1. Spoon yogurt into 4 individual cups.
2. Sprinkle 2 tbsp. walnuts over each and drizzle 2 tsp. honey over each.
3. Top with fruit or granola, whichever is preferred.

Nutrition:
- Calories: 300.
- Fat: 10 g.
- Carbs: 25 g.
- Protein: 29 g.

13. Tahini Pine Nuts Toast

Level of difficulty: Novice level
Preparation Time: 5 minutes.
Cooking Time: 0 minutes.
Servings: 2

Ingredients:
- 2 whole-wheat bread slices, toasted.
- 1 tsp. water.
- 1 tbsp. tahini paste.
- 2 tsp. feta cheese, crumbled.
- Juice of ½ lemon.
- 2 tsp. pine nuts.
- A pinch of black pepper.

Directions:
1. In a bowl, mix the tahini with the water and the lemon juice, whisk well, and spread over the toasted bread slices.
2. Top each serving with the remaining ingredients and serve for breakfast.

Nutrition:
- Calories: 142.
- Fat: 7.6 g.
- Carbs: 13.7 g.
- Protein: 5.8 g.

14. Feta Avocado and Mashed Chickpea Toast

Level of difficulty: Intermediate
Preparation Time: 10 minutes.
Cooking Time: 15 minutes.
Servings: 4
Ingredients:
- 15 oz. can chickpeas.
- 2 oz. (½ cup) diced feta cheese.
- 1 pitted avocado.
- 2 tsp. lemon (or 1 tbsp. orange).
- ½ tsp. black pepper.
- 2 tsp. honey.
- 4 slices multigrain toast.

Directions:
1. Toast the bread. Drain the chickpeas in a colander. Scoop the avocado flesh into the bowl. Use a large fork/potato masher to mash them until the mix is spreadable.
2. Pour in the lemon juice, pepper, and feta. Combine and divide onto the four slices of toast. Drizzle using the honey and serve.

Nutrition:
- Calories: 337
- Carbs: 43 g.
- Fat: 13 g.
- Protein: 13 g.

15. Feta Frittata

Level of difficulty: Novice level
Preparation Time: 15 minutes.
Cooking Time: 25 minutes.
Servings: 2
Ingredients:
- 1 small clove garlic.
- 1 green onion.
- 2 large eggs.
- ½ cup egg substitute.
- 4 tbsp. crumbled feta cheese, divided.
- 1/3 Cup plum tomato.
- 4 thin avocado slices.
- 2 tbsp. reduced-fat sour cream.
- 6-inch skillet.

Directions:
1. Thinly slice/mince the onion, garlic, and tomato. Peel the avocado before slicing. Heat the pan using the medium temperature setting and spritz it with cooking oil.
2. Whisk the egg substitute, eggs, and the feta cheese. Add the egg mixture into the pan. Cover and simmer for 4 to 6 minutes.
3. Sprinkle it using the rest of the feta cheese and tomato. Cover and continue cooking until the eggs are set or about 2 to 3 more minutes.

4. Wait for about five minutes before cutting it into halves. Serve with avocado and sour cream.

Nutrition:
- Calories: 460.
- Carbs: 8 g.
- Fat: 37 g.
- Protein: 24 g.

16. Pilaf with Cream Cheese

Level of difficulty: Novice level
Preparation Time: 11 minutes
Cooking Time: 34 minutes
Servings: 6
Ingredients:
- 2 cups yellow long grain rice, parboiled
- 1 cup onion
- 4 green onions
- 3 tbsp. butter
- 3 tbsp. vegetable broth
- 2 teaspoons cayenne pepper
- 1 teaspoon paprika
- ½ teaspoon cloves, minced
- 2 tbsp. mint leaves
- 1 bunch fresh mint leaves to garnish
- 1 tbsp. olive oil

Cheese Cream:
- 3 tbsp. olive oil
- sea salt & black pepper to taste
- 9 ounces cream cheese

Directions:
1. Start by heating your oven to 360, and then get out a pan. Heat your butter and olive oil together, and cook your onions and spring onions for two minutes.
2. Add in your salt, pepper, paprika, cloves, vegetable broth, rice and remaining seasoning.
3. Sauté for three minutes.
4. Wrap with foil, and bake for another half hour. Allow it to cool.
5. Mix in the cream cheese, cheese, olive oil, salt and pepper. Serve your pilaf garnished with fresh mint leaves.

Nutrition:
- 364 Calories
- 5g Protein
- 30g Fat
- 12g Carbohydrates

17. Easy Spaghetti Squash

Level of difficulty: Novice level
Preparation Time: 13 minutes
Cooking Time: 45 minutes
Servings: 6
Ingredients:
- 2 spring onions, chopped fine
- 3 cloves garlic, minced
- 1 zucchini, diced
- 1 red bell pepper, diced
- 1 tbsp. Italian seasoning
- 1 tomato, small & chopped fine
- 1 tbsp. parsley, fresh & chopped
- pinch lemon pepper
- dash sea salt, fine
- 4 ounces feta cheese, crumbled
- 3 Italian sausage links, casing removed
- 2 tbsp. olive oil
- 1 spaghetti sauce, halved lengthwise

Directions:
1. Prep oven to 350, and get out a large baking sheet. Coat it with cooking spray, and then put your squash on it with the cut side down.
2. Bake at 350 for forty-five minutes. It should be tender.
3. Turn the squash over, and bake for five more minutes. Scrape the strands into a larger bowl.

4. Cook tbsp. of olive oil in a skillet, and then add in your Italian sausage. Cook at eight minutes before removing it and placing it in a bowl.
5. Add another tbsp. of olive oil to the skillet and cook your garlic and onions until softened. This will take five minutes. Throw in your Italian seasoning, red peppers and zucchini. Cook for another five minutes. Your vegetables should be softened.
6. Mix in your feta cheese and squash, cooking until the cheese has melted.
7. Stir in your sausage, and then season with lemon pepper and salt. Serve with parsley and tomato.

Nutrition:
- 423 Calories
- 18g Protein
- 30g Fat
- 15g Carbohydrates

18. Roasted Eggplant Salad

Level of difficulty: Novice level
Preparation Time: 14 minutes
Cooking Time: 36 minutes
Servings: 6
Ingredients:
- 1 red onion, sliced
- 2 tbsp. parsley
- 1 teaspoon thyme
- 2 cups cherry tomatoes
- 1 teaspoon oregano
- 3 tbsp. olive oil
- 1 teaspoon basil
- 3 eggplants, peeled & cubed

Directions:
1. Start by heating your oven to 350.
2. Season your eggplant with basil, salt, pepper, oregano, thyme and olive oil.
3. Arrange it on a baking tray, and bake for a half hour.
4. Toss with your remaining ingredients before serving.

Nutrition:
- 148 Calories
- 3.5g Protein
- 7.7g Fat
- 13g Carbohydrates

19. Smoked Salmon and Poached Eggs on Toast

Level of difficulty: Novice level
Preparation Time: 10 minutes.
Cooking Time: 4 minutes.
Servings: 4
Ingredients:
- 2 oz. avocado smashed.
- 2 slices of bread toasted.
- Pinch of kosher salt and cracked black pepper.
- ¼ tsp. freshly squeezed lemon juice.
- 2 eggs see notes, poached.
- 3.5 oz. smoked salmon.
- 1 tbsp. thinly sliced scallions.
- Splash of Kikkoman soy sauce optional.
- Microgreens are optional.

Directions:
1. Take a small bowl and then smash the avocado into it. Then, add the lemon juice and also a pinch of salt into the mixture. Then, mix it well and set aside.
2. After that, poach the eggs and toast the bread for some time. Once the bread is toasted, you will have to spread the avocado on both slices and after that, add the smoked salmon to each slice.
3. Thereafter, carefully transfer the poached eggs to the respective toasts. Add a splash of Kikkoman soy sauce and some cracked pepper; then, just garnish with scallions and microgreens.

Nutrition:
- Calories: 459.
- Protein: 31 g.
- Fat: 22 g.
- Carbs: 33 g.

20. Honey Almond Ricotta Spread With Peaches

Level of difficulty: Intermediate
Preparation Time: 5 minutes.
Cooking Time: 8 minutes.
Servings: 4
Ingredients:
- ½ cup fisher sliced almonds.
- 1 cup whole milk ricotta.
- ¼ tsp. almond extract.
- Zest from an orange, optional.
- 1 tsp. honey.
- Hearty whole-grain toast.
- English muffin or bagel.
- Extra fisher sliced almonds.
- Sliced peaches.
- Extra honey for drizzling.
- Olive oil.

Directions:
1. Cut peaches into a proper shape and then brush them with olive oil. After that, set it aside. Take a bowl; combine the ingredients for the filling. Set aside.
2. Then just preheat the grill to medium. Place peaches cut side down onto the greased grill. Close lid cover and then just grill until the peaches have softened, approximately 6 to 10 minutes, depending on the size of the peaches.
3. Then you will have to place peach halves onto a serving plate. Put about 1 tbsp. ricotta mixture into the cavity (you are also allowed to use a small scooper).
4. Sprinkle it with slivered almonds, crushed amaretti cookies, and honey. Decorate with the mint leaves.

Nutrition:
- Calories: 187.
- Protein: 7 g.
- Fat: 9 g.
- Carbs: 18 g.

21. Mediterranean Eggs Cups

Level of difficulty: Novice level
Preparation Time: 10 minutes.
Cooking Time: 20 minutes.
Servings: 8
Ingredients:
- 1 cup spinach, finely diced.
- 4 large basil leaves, finely diced.
- Pepper and salt to taste.
- 8 large eggs.
- Bell peppers

Directions:
1. Warm the oven to 375° F. Then, roll the dough sheet into a 12x8-inch rectangle. Then, cut in half lengthwise.
2. After that, you will have to cut each half crosswise into 4 pieces, forming 8 (4x3-inch) pieces of dough. Then, press each into the bottom and up sides of the ungreased muffin cup.
3. Trim dough to keep the dough from touching, if essential. Set aside. Then, you will have to combine the eggs, salt, pepper in the bowl and beat it with a whisk until well mixed. Set aside.
4. Melt the butter in a 12-inch skillet over medium heat until sizzling; add bell peppers. You will have to cook it, stirring occasionally for 2 to 3 minutes or until crisply tender.
5. After that, add spinach leaves; continue cooking until spinach is wilted. Then just add egg mixture and prosciutto.

6. Divide the mixture evenly among prepared muffin cups. Finally, bake it for 14 to 17 minutes or until the crust is golden brown.

Nutrition:
- Calories: 240.
- Protein: 9 g.
- Fat: 16 g.
- Carbs: 13 g.

22. Low-Carb Baked Eggs with Avocado and Feta

Level of difficulty: Novice level
Preparation Time: 10 minutes.
Cooking Time: 15 minutes.
Servings: 2
Ingredients:
- 1 avocado.
- 4 eggs.
- 2 or 3 tbsp. crumbled feta cheese.
- Nonstick cooking spray.
- Pepper and salt to taste.

Directions:
1. First, you will have to preheat the oven to 400° F. After that, when the oven is at the proper temperature, you will have to put the gratin dishes right on the baking sheet.
2. Then, leave the dishes to heat in the oven for almost 10 minutes after that process, you need to break the eggs into individual ramekins.
3. Then, let the avocado and eggs come to room temperature for at least 10 minutes. Then, peel the avocado properly and cut it each half into 6 to 8 slices.
4. You will have to remove the dishes from the oven and spray them with the non-stick spray. Then, you will have to arrange all the sliced avocados in the dishes and tip 2eggs into each dish. Sprinkle with feta, add pepper and salt to taste. Serve.

Nutrition:
- Calories: 280.
- Protein: 11 g.
- Fat: 23 g.
- Carbs: 10 g.

23. Mediterranean Eggs White Breakfast Sandwich with Roasted Tomatoes

Level of difficulty: Novice level
Preparation Time: 15 minutes.
Cooking Time: 10 minutes.
Servings: 2
Ingredients:
- Salt and pepper to taste.
- ¼ cup egg whites.
- 1 tsp. chopped fresh herbs like rosemary, basil, parsley.
- 1 whole-grain seeded ciabatta roll.
- 1 tsp. butter.
- 1 or 2 slices Muenster cheese.
- 1 tbsp. pesto.
- About ½ cup roasted tomatoes.
- 10 oz. grape tomatoes.
- 1 tbsp. extra-virgin olive oil.

Directions:
1. First, you will have to melt the butter over medium heat in the small nonstick skillet. Then, mix the egg whites with pepper and salt.
2. Then, sprinkle it with fresh herbs. After that cook it for almost 3 to 4 minutes or until the eggs are done, then flip it carefully.
3. Meanwhile, toast ciabatta bread in the toaster. Place the egg on the bottom half of the sandwich rolls, then top with cheese

4. Add roasted tomatoes and the top half of the roll. To make a roasted tomato, preheat the oven to 400° F. Then, slice the tomatoes in half lengthwise.
5. Place on the baking sheet and drizzle with olive oil. Season it with pepper and salt and then roast in the oven for about 20 minutes. Skins will appear wrinkled when done.

Nutrition:
- Calories: 458.
- Protein: 21 g.
- Fat: 24 g.
- Carbs: 51 g.

24. Mediterranean Feta and Quinoa Egg Muffins

Level of difficulty: Novice level
Preparation Time: 15 minutes.
Cooking Time: 15 minutes.
Servings: 12
Ingredients:
- 2 cups baby spinach finely chopped.
- 1 cup chopped or sliced cherry tomatoes.
- ½ cup finely chopped onion.
- 1 tbsp. chopped fresh oregano.
- 1 cup crumbled feta cheese.
- ½ cup chopped (pitted) kalamata olives.
- 2 tsp. high oleic sunflower oil.
- 1 cup cooked quinoa.
- 8 eggs.
- ¼ tsp. salt.

Directions:
1. Preheat oven to 350° F and then prepare 12 silicone muffin holders on the baking sheet, or just grease a 12-cup muffin tin with oil and set aside.
2. Finely chop the vegetables and then heat the skillet to medium. After that, add the vegetable oil and onions and sauté for 2 minutes.
3. Then, add tomatoes and sauté for another minute, then add spinach and sauté until wilted, about 1 minute.
4. Place the beaten egg into a bowl and then add lots of vegetables like feta cheese, quinoa, veggie mixture as well as salt, and then stir well until everything is properly combined.
5. Pour the ready mixture into greased muffin tins or silicone cups, dividing the mixture equally. Then, bake it in an oven for 30 minutes or so.

Nutrition:
- Calories: 113.
- Protein: 6 g.
- Fat: 7 g.
- Carbs: 5 g.

25. Bacon and Brie Omelet Wedges

Level of difficulty: Novice level
Preparation Time: 10 minutes.
Cooking Time: 10 minutes.
Servings: 6
Ingredients:
- 2 tbsp. olive oil.
- 7 oz. smoked bacon.
- 6 beaten eggs.
- Small bunch chives, snipped.
- 3 ½ oz. brie, sliced.
- 1 tsp. red wine vinegar.
- 1 tsp. Dijon mustard.
- 1 cucumber, halved, deseeded and sliced diagonally.
- 7 oz. radish, quartered.
- Pepper.

Directions:
1. Turn your grill on and set it too high. Take a small-sized pan and add 1 tsp.

oil, allow the oil to heat up. Add lardons and fry until crisp. Drain the lardon on kitchen paper.
2. Take another non-stick cast iron frying pan and place it over the grill, heat 2 tsp. oil. Add lardons, eggs, chives, ground pepper to the frying pan. Cook on low until they are semi-set.
3. Carefully lay brie on top and grill until the brie sets and is a golden texture. Remove it from the pan and cut it up into wedges.
4. Take a small bowl and create dressing by mixing olive oil, mustard, vinegar and seasoning. Add cucumber to the bowl and mix, serve alongside the omelet wedges.

Nutrition:
- Calories: 35.
- Fat: 31 g.
- Carbs: 3 g.
- Protein: 25 g.

26. Pastry-Less Spanakopita

Level of difficulty: Novice level
Preparation Time: 5 minutes.
Cooking Time: 20 minutes.
Servings: 4
Ingredients:
- 1/8 Tsp. black pepper, add as per taste.
- 1/3 Cup of extra virgin olive oil.
- 4 lightly beaten eggs.
- 7 cups of lettuce, preferably a spring mix (mesclun).
- ½ cup of crumbled feta cheese.
- 1/8 Tsp. of sea salt, add to taste.
- 1 finely chopped medium yellow onion.

Directions:
1. Warm the oven to 180° C and grease the flan dish. Once done, pour the extra virgin olive oil into a large saucepan and heat it over medium heat with the onions, until they are translucent.
2. Add greens and keep stirring until all the ingredients are wilted. Season it with salt and pepper and transfer the greens to the prepared dish and sprinkle on some feta cheese.
3. Pour the eggs and bake it for 20 minutes till it is cooked through and slightly brown.

Nutrition:
- Calories: 325.
- Protein: 11.2 g.
- Fat: 27.9 g.
- Carbs: 7.3 g.

27. Date and Walnut Overnight Oats

Level of difficulty: Novice level
Preparation Time: 5 minutes.
Cooking Time: 20 minutes.
Servings: 2
Ingredients:
- ¼ cup Greek yogurt, plain.
- 1/3 Cup of yogurt.
- 2/3 Cup of oats.
- 1 cup of milk.
- 2 tsp. date syrup. You can also use maple syrup or honey.
- 1 mashed banana.
- ¼ tsp. cinnamon.
- ¼ cup walnuts.
- Pinch of salt (approx 1/8 tsp.)

Directions:
1. Firstly, get a mason jar or a small bowl and add all the ingredients. After that stir and mix all the ingredients well. Cover it securely, and cool it in a refrigerator overnight.

2. After that, take it out the next morning, add more liquid or cinnamon if required, and serve cold. (However, you can also microwave it for people with a warmer palate.)

Nutrition:
- Calories: 350.
- Protein: 14 g.
- Fat: 12 g.
- Carbs: 49 g.

28. Pear and Mango Smoothie

Level of difficulty: Novice level
Preparation Time: 5 minutes.
Cooking Time: 0 minutes.
Servings: 1
Ingredients:
- 1 ripe mango, cored and chopped.
- ½ pear, peeled, pitted and chopped.
- 1 cup kale, chopped.
- ½ cup plain Greek yogurt.
- 2 ice cubes.

Directions:
1. Add pear, mango, yogurt, kale, and mango to a blender and puree. Add ice and blend until you have a smooth texture. Serve and enjoy!

Nutrition:
- Calories: 293.
- Fat: 8 g.
- Carbs: 53 g.
- Protein: 8 g.

29. Eggplant Salad

Level of difficulty: Novice level
Preparation Time: 20 minutes.
Cooking Time: 15 minutes.
Servings: 8
Ingredients:
- 1 large eggplant, washed and cubed.
- 1 tomato, seeded and chopped.
- 1 small onion, diced.
- 2 tbsp. parsley, chopped.
- 2 tbsp. extra virgin olive oil.
- 2 tbsp. distilled white vinegar.
- ½ cup feta cheese, crumbled.
- Salt as needed.

Directions:
1. Preheat your outdoor grill to medium-high. Pierce the eggplant a few times using a knife/fork. Cook the eggplants on your grill for about 15 minutes until they are charred.
2. Keep it on the side and allow them to cool. Remove the skin from the eggplant and dice the pulp. Transfer the pulp to a mixing bowl and add parsley, onion, tomato, olive oil, feta cheese and vinegar.
3. Mix well and chill for 1 hour. Season with salt and enjoy!

Nutrition:
- Calories: 99.
- Fat: 7 g.
- Carbs: 7 g.
- Protein: 3.4 g.

30. Artichoke Frittata

Level of difficulty: Novice level
Preparation Time: 5 minutes.
Cooking Time: 10 minutes.
Servings: 4
Ingredients:
- 8 large eggs.
- ¼ cup asiago cheese, grated.
- 1 tbsp. fresh basil, chopped.
- 1 tsp. fresh oregano, chopped.
- Pinch of sea salt and pepper.
- 1 tsp. extra virgin olive oil.
- 1 tsp. garlic, minced.
- 1 cup canned artichokes, drained.
- 1 tomato, chopped.

Directions:
1. Preheat your oven to broil. Take a medium bowl and whisk in eggs, asiago cheese, oregano, basil, sea salt and pepper. Blend in a bowl.
2. Place a large ovenproof skillet over medium-high heat and add olive oil. Add garlic and sauté for 1 minute. Remove skillet from heat and pour in the egg mix.
3. Return skillet to heat and sprinkle artichoke hearts and tomato over eggs. Cook frittata without stirring for 8 minutes.
4. Place skillet under the broiler for 1 minute until the top is lightly browned. Cut frittata into 4 pieces and serve. Enjoy!

Nutrition:
- Calories: 199.
- Fat: 13 g.
- Carbs: 5 g.
- Protein: 16 g.

31. Orange Fish Meal

Level of difficulty: Intermediate
Preparation Time: 10 minutes
Cooking Time: 5 minutes
Servings: 4
Ingredients:
- ¼ teaspoon kosher or sea salt
- 1 tbsp. extra-virgin olive oil
- 1 tbsp. orange juice
- 4 (4-ounce) tilapia fillets, with or without skin
- ¼ cup chopped red onion
- 1 avocado, pitted, skinned, and sliced

Directions:
1. Take a baking dish of 9-inch; add olive oil, orange juice, and salt. Combine well. Add fish fillets and coat well.
2. Add onions over fish fillets. Cover with a plastic wrap. Microwave for 3 minutes until fish is cooked well and easy to flake. Serve warm with sliced avocado on top.

Nutrition:
- 231 Calories
- 9g Fat
- 2.5g Protein
- 3.8g Carbohydrates

32. Shrimp Zoodles

Level of difficulty: Novice level
Preparation Time: 10 minutes
Cooking Time: 5 minutes
Servings: 2
Ingredients:
- 2 tbsp. chopped parsley
- 2 teaspoons minced garlic
- 1 teaspoon salt
- ½ teaspoon black pepper
- 2 medium zucchinis, spiralized
- 3/4 pounds medium shrimp, peeled & deveined
- 1 tbsp. olive oil
- 1 lemon, juiced and zested

Directions:
1. Take a medium saucepan or skillet, add oil, lemon juice, lemon zest. Heat over medium heat. Add shrimps and stir-cook 1 minute per side.
2. Sauté garlic and red pepper flakes for 1 more minute. Add Zoodles and stir gently; cook for 3 minutes until cooked to satisfaction. Season well, serve warm with parsley on top.

Nutrition:
- 329 Calories
- 12g Fat
- 3g Protein
- 6.5g Carbohydrates

33. Asparagus Trout Meal

Level of difficulty: Novice level
Preparation Time: 10 minutes
Cooking Time: 20 minutes
Servings: 4
Ingredients:

- 2 pounds trout fillets
- 1-pound asparagus
- 1 tbsp. olive oil
- 1 garlic clove, finely minced
- 1 scallion, thinly sliced
- 4 medium golden potatoes
- 2 Roma tomatoes, chopped
- 8 pitted kalamata olives, chopped
- 1 large carrot, thinly sliced
- 2 tbsp. dried parsley
- ¼ cup ground cumin
- 2 tbsp. paprika
- 1 tbsp. vegetable bouillon seasoning
- ½ cup dry white wine

Directions:
1. In a mixing bowl, add fish fillets, white pepper and salt. Combine to mix well with each other. Take a medium saucepan or skillet, add oil.
2. Heat over medium heat. Add asparagus, potatoes, garlic, white part scallion, and stir-cook until become softened for 4-5 minutes. Add tomatoes, carrot and olives; stir-cook for 6-7 minutes until turn tender. Add cumin, paprika, parsley, bouillon seasoning, and salt. Stir mixture well.
3. Mix in white wine and fish fillets. Over low heat, cover and simmer mixture for about 6 minutes until fish is easy to flake, stir in between. Serve warm with green scallions on top.

Nutrition:
- 303 Calories
- 17g Fat
- 6g Protein
- 5g Carbohydrates

34. Mediterranean Lentil Sloppy Joes

Level of difficulty: Novice level
Preparation Time: 5 minutes
Cooking Time: 15 minutes
Servings: 4
Ingredients:

- 1 tbsp. extra-virgin olive oil
- 1 cup chopped onion
- 1 cup chopped bell pepper
- 2 garlic cloves
- 1 (15-ounce) can lentils, drained and rinsed
- 1 (14.5-ounce) can low-sodium tomatoes
- 1 teaspoon ground cumin
- 1 teaspoon dried thyme
- ¼ teaspoon kosher or sea salt
- 4 whole-wheat pita breads, split open
- 1½ cups chopped seedless cucumber
- 1 cup chopped romaine lettuce

Directions:
1. In a saucepan at medium-high heat, sauté onion and bell pepper for 4 minutes. Cook garlic and stir in lentils,

tomatoes (with their liquid), cumin, thyme, and salt.
2. Turn the heat to medium and cook, stirring occasionally, for 10 minutes.
3. Stuff the lentil mixture inside each pita. Lay the cucumbers and lettuce on top of mixture and serve.

Nutrition:
- 334 Calories
- 5g Fat
- 16g Protein
- 2.5g Carbohydrates

35. Gorgonzola Sweet Potato Burgers

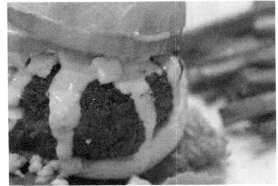

Level of difficulty: Novice level
Preparation Time: 10 minutes
Cooking Time: 15 minutes
Servings: 4
Ingredients:
- 1 large sweet potato (about 8 ounces)
- 2 tbsp. extra-virgin olive oil, divided
- 1 cup chopped onion (about ½ medium onion)
- 1 cup old-fashioned rolled oats
- 1 large egg
- 1 tbsp. balsamic vinegar
- 1 tbsp. dried oregano
- 1 garlic clove
- ¼ teaspoon kosher or sea salt
- ½ cup crumbled Gorgonzola

Directions:
1. Prick sweet potato all over and microwave on high for 4 to 5 minutes. Cool slightly, then slice in half.
2. While the sweet potato is cooking, in a large skillet over medium-high heat, heat 1 tbsp. of oil. Cook onion
3. Using a spoon, carefully scoop the sweet potato flesh out of the skin and put the flesh in a food processor. Blend onion, oats, egg, vinegar, oregano, garlic, and salt. Add the cheese and pulse four times to barely combine. With your hands, form the mixture into four (½-cup-size) burgers. Place the burgers on a plate, and press to flatten each to about ¾-inch thick.
4. Clean out the skillet with a paper towel, then heat the remaining 1 tbsp. of oil over medium-high heat until very hot, about 2 minutes. Add the burgers to the hot oil, then turn the heat down to medium. Cook the burgers for 5 minutes, flip with a spatula, then cook an additional 5 minutes. Enjoy as is or serve on salad greens or whole-wheat rolls.

Nutrition:
- 223 Calories
- 13g Fat
- 7g Protein
- 8.6g Carbohydrates

36. Zucchini-Eggplant Gratin

Level of difficulty: Novice level
Preparation Time: 10 minutes
Cooking Time: 20 minutes
Servings: 6
Ingredients:
- 1 large eggplant
- 2 large zucchinis
- ¼ teaspoon black pepper

- ¼ teaspoon kosher or sea salt
- 3 tbsp. extra-virgin olive oil
- 1 tbsp. all-purpose flour
- ¾ cup 2% milk
- 1/3 cup Parmesan cheese
- 1 cup chopped tomato
- 1 cup diced or shredded fresh mozzarella
- ¼ cup fresh basil leaves

Directions:
1. Preheat the oven to 425°F.
2. Mix eggplant, zucchini, pepper, and salt.
3. Situate skillet over medium-high heat, heat 1 tbsp. of oil. Add half the veggie mixture to the skillet. Stir a few times, then cover and cook for 5 minutes, stirring occasionally. Pour the cooked veggies into a baking dish. Situate skillet back on the heat, add 1 tbsp. of oil, and repeat with the remaining veggies. Add the veggies to the baking dish.
4. While the vegetables are cooking, heat the milk in the microwave for 1 minute. Set aside.
5. Place a medium saucepan over medium heat. Add the remaining tbsp. of oil and flour, and whisk together for about 1 minute
6. Slowly pour the warm milk into the oil mixture, whisking the entire time. Add 1/3 cup of Parmesan cheese, and whisk until melted. Pour the cheese sauce over the vegetables in the baking dish and mix well.
7. Gently mix in the tomatoes and mozzarella cheese. Roast in the oven for 10 minutes, or until the gratin is almost set and not runny. Garnish with the fresh basil leaves and the remaining 2 tbsp. of Parmesan cheese before serving.

Nutrition:
- 207 Calories
- 14g Fat
- 11g Protein
- 4.8g Carbohydrates

37. Chicken Gyros with Tzatziki Sauce

Level of difficulty: Novice level
Preparation Time: 15 minutes
Cooking Time: 10 minutes
Servings: 2
Ingredients:
- 2 tbsp. freshly squeezed lemon juice
- 2 tbsp. olive oil, divided, plus more for oiling the grill
- 1 teaspoon minced fresh oregano
- ½ teaspoon garlic powder
- Salt, to taste
- 8 ounces (227 g) chicken tenders
- 1 small eggplant, cut into 1-inch strips lengthwise
- 1 small zucchini, cut into ½-inch strips lengthwise
- ½ red pepper, seeded and cut in half lengthwise

- ½ English cucumber, peeled and minced
- ¾ cup plain Greek yogurt
- 1 tbsp. minced fresh dill
- 2 (8-inch) pita breads

Directions:
1. Combine the lemon juice, 1 tbsp. of olive oil, oregano, garlic powder, and salt in a medium bowl. Add the chicken and let marinate for 30 minutes.
2. Place the eggplant, zucchini, and red pepper in a large mixing bowl and sprinkle with salt and the remaining 1 tbsp. of olive oil. Toss well to coat. Let the vegetables rest while the chicken is marinating.
3. Make the tzatziki sauce: Combine the cucumber, yogurt, salt, and dill in a medium bowl. Stir well to incorporate and set aside in the refrigerator.
4. When ready, preheat the grill to medium-high heat and oil the grill grates.
5. Drain any liquid from the vegetables and put them on the grill.
6. Remove the chicken tenders from the marinade and put them on the grill.
7. Grill the chicken and vegetables for 3 minutes per side, or until the chicken is no longer pink inside.
8. Remove the chicken and vegetables from the grill and set aside. On the grill, heat the pitas for about 30 seconds, flipping them frequently.
9. Divide the chicken tenders and vegetables between the pitas and top each with ¼ cup of the prepared sauce. Roll the pitas up like a cone and serve.

Nutrition:
- Calories: 586
- Fat: 21.9g
- Protein: 39.0g
- Carbs: 62.0g
- Fiber: 11.8g
- Sodium: 955mg

38. Crispy Pesto Chicken

Level of difficulty: Intermediate
Preparation Time: 15 minutes
Cooking Time: 50 minutes
Servings: 2

Ingredients:
- 12 ounces (340 g) small red potatoes (3 or 4 potatoes), scrubbed and diced into 1-inch pieces
- 1 tbsp. olive oil
- ½ teaspoon garlic powder
- ¼ teaspoon salt
- 1 (8-ounce / 227-g) boneless, skinless chicken breast
- 3 tbsp. prepared pesto

Directions:
1. Heat your oven to 425°F (220°C). Line a baking sheet with parchment paper.
2. Combine the potatoes, olive oil, garlic powder, and salt in a medium bowl. Toss well to coat.
3. Arrange the potatoes on the parchment paper and roast for 10 minutes. Flip the potatoes and roast for an additional 10 minutes.
4. Meanwhile, put the chicken in the same bowl and toss with the pesto, coating the chicken evenly.
5. Check the potatoes to make sure they are golden brown on the top and bottom. Toss them again and add the chicken breast to the pan.
6. Turn the heat down to 350°F (180°C) and roast the chicken and potatoes for 30 minutes. Check to make sure the chicken reaches an internal temperature of 165°F (74°C) and the potatoes are fork-tender.

7. Let cool for 5 minutes before serving.

Nutrition:
- Calories: 378
- Fat: 16.0g
- Protein: 29.8g
- Carbs: 30.1g
- Fiber: 4.0g
- Sodium: 425mg

39. Beef Stew with Beans and Zucchini

Level of difficulty: Novice level
Preparation Time: 20 minutes
Cooking Time: 6 to 8 hours
Servings: 2
Ingredients:
- 1 (15-ounce / 425-g) can diced or crushed tomatoes with basil
- 1 teaspoon beef base
- 2 tbsp. olive oil, divided
- 8 ounces (227 g) baby bella (cremini) mushrooms, quartered
- 2 garlic cloves, minced
- ½ large onion, diced
- 1 pound (454 g) cubed beef stew meat
- 3 tbsp. flour
- ¼ teaspoon salt
- Pinch freshly ground black pepper
- ¾ cup dry red wine
- ¼ cup minced brined olives
- 1 fresh rosemary sprig
- 1 (15-ounce / 425-g) can white cannellini beans, drained and rinsed
- One medium zucchini, cut in half lengthwise and then cut into 1-inch pieces.

Directions:
1. Place the tomatoes into a slow cooker and set it to low heat. Add the beef base and stir to incorporate.
2. Heat 1 tbsp. of olive oil in a large sauté pan over medium heat.
3. Add the mushrooms and onion and sauté for 10 minutes, stirring occasionally, or until they're golden.
4. Add the garlic and cook for 30 seconds more. Transfer the vegetables to the slow cooker.
5. In a plastic food storage bag, combine the stew meat with the flour, salt, and pepper. Seal the bag & shake well to combine.
6. Heat the remaining 1 tbsp. of olive oil in the sauté pan over high heat.
7. Add the floured meat and sear to get a crust on the outside edges. Deglaze the pan by adding about half of the red wine and scraping up any browned bits on the bottom. Stir so the wine thickens a bit and transfer to the slow cooker along with any remaining wine.
8. Stir the stew to incorporate the ingredients. Stir in the olives and rosemary, cover, and cook for 6 to 8 hours on Low.
9. About 30 minutes before the stew is finished, add the beans and zucchini to let them warm through. Serve warm.

Nutrition:
- Calories: 389
- Fat: 15.1g
- Protein: 30.8g
- Carbs: 25.0g
- Fiber: 8.0g
- Sodium: 582mg

40. Tomato Salad

Level of difficulty: Novice level
Preparation Time: 22 minutes
Cooking Time: 0 minute
Servings: 4

Ingredients:
- 1 cucumber, sliced
- ¼ cup sun dried tomatoes, chopped
- 1 lb. tomatoes, cubed
- ½ cup black olives
- 1 red onion, sliced
- 1 tbsp. balsamic vinegar
- ¼ cup parsley, fresh & chopped
- 2 tbsp. olive oil

Directions:
Get out a bowl and combine all of your vegetables together. To make your dressing mix all your seasoning, olive oil and vinegar.
1. Toss with your salad and serve fresh.

Nutrition:
- 126 Calories
- 2.1g Protein
- 9.2g Fat
- 5.6g Carbohydrates

CHAPTER 3. LUNCH

41. Beef Kofta

Level of difficulty: Novice level
Preparation Time: 10 minutes
Cooking Time: 20 minutes
Servings: 4
Ingredients:
- Olive oil cooking spray
- ½ onion, roughly chopped
- 1-inch piece ginger, peeled
- 2 garlic cloves, peeled
- 1/3 cup fresh parsley
- 1/3 cup fresh mint
- 1 pound ground beef
- 1 tbsp. ground cumin
- 1 tbsp. ground coriander
- 1 teaspoon ground cinnamon
- ¾ teaspoon kosher salt
- ½ teaspoon ground sumac
- ¼ teaspoon ground cloves
- ¼ teaspoon freshly ground black pepper

Directions:
1. Preheat the oven to 400°F. Grease a 12-cup muffin tin with olive oil cooking spray.
2. In a food processor, add the onion, ginger, garlic, parsley, and mint; process until minced.
3. Place the onion mixture in a large bowl. Add the beef, cumin, coriander, cinnamon, salt, sumac, cloves, and black pepper and mix together thoroughly with your hands.
4. Divide the beef mixture into 12 balls and place each one in a cup of the prepared muffin tin. Bake for 20 minutes.

Nutrition:
- Calories: 280
- Carbs: 0g
- Fat: 12.5g
- Protein: 29g

42. Herb Roasted Lamb Chops

Level of difficulty: Novice level
Preparation Time: 10 minutes
Cooking Time: 20 minutes

Servings: 4
Ingredients
- 3 tbsp. extra virgin olive oil
- 8 lamb chops
- 2 garlic cloves, cut into small slices
- Kosher salt, to taste
- 2 tbsp. freshly rosemary leaves

Directions:
1. Preheat oven to 375°F.
2. Place chops on rack in a baking sheet. Brush chops with olive oil.
3. Cut 1 small, shallow slit in the top of each lamb chop.
4. Place a sliver of garlic in each cut.
5. Season lamb with salt and sprinkle with rosemary.
6. Roast chops 20 minutes or until an instant-read thermometer inserted in the thickest part of the chop registers 160°F for medium.
7. Serve warm. Enjoy!

Nutrition:
- Calories: 280
- Carbs: 0g
- Fat: 12.5g
- Protein: 29g

43. Grilled Salmon with Lemon and Wine

Level of difficulty: Novice level

Preparation Time: 10 minutes
Cooking Time: 10 minutes

Servings: 4
Ingredients:
- 1 big lemon
- 1 ½ cup of olive oil
- ½ tsp. pepper
- 3 tsp of vegetable oil
- 4 of 6 oz. of salmon fillets
- 1 tsp. lime zest
- 1 ½ tbsp. salt

Directions:
1. Prepare the grill and rub the fillets with oil.
2. Put lime zest, lemon zest, salt, and pepper on both sides of fillets.
3. Brush oil on the grill, put the salmon and the fillets on the grill, and allow it to grill for about 7 minutes, turn it to the other side and grill for about 3 minutes.
4. The salmon can now be served with lemon wedges.

Nutrition:
- Calories: 270
- Carbs: 11.5g
- Fat: 14.2g
- Protein: 28.1g

44. Beer-batter Fish

Level of difficulty: Novice level
Preparation Time: 5 minutes
Cooking Time: 60 minutes
Servings: 4
Ingredients:
- 1 ¼ Tbsp. of salt

- 1 ½ cups of dark beer, cold
- ¾ cup of all-purpose flour
- 1 Tbsp. of baking powder
- ¾ cup of cornstarch
- 4 of 6 oz. of cod fillets
- 3-4 pieces of sunflower oil

Directions:
1. Get a large bowl, put cornstarch, ½ Tbsp. of salt, leaven, flour. Then mix all of them in beer to get to the purpose of batter.
2. Put the batter inside the refrigerator.
3. Wash your fish and put it on parchment paper, add half Tbsp. of salt.
4. Put oil inside a frying pan, put the fish inside the oil and fry it, till it's golden in color.
5. Remove the fish after frying and put it inside oil to soak.
6. Add the remaining half Tbsp. of salt and serve.

Nutrition:
- Calories: 250kcal
- Carbs: 20g
- Fat: 12g
- Protein: 14g

45. Sole with Spinach

Level of difficulty: Novice level
Preparation Time: 5 minutes
Cooking Time: 20 minutes
Servings: 4
Ingredients:
- 4 (6-oz) of sole fillets
- 4 scallions with ends trimmed and sliced
- 1 pound package of frozen spinach (thawed)
- 1 tsp of salt
- 3tsps. of chopped fennel
- ½ tsp pepper
- 1tsp sweet paprika
- 2 Tbsp. of lemon

Directions:
1. Preheat the oven to 400F
2. Place a little pan over medium heat and add 2 Tbsp. of oil and warmth for 3o seconds.
3. Add the scallion and cook for 3-4 minutes; allow it to chill.
4. In a bowl, add scallion, spinach, pepper, 1/2tsp of salt, and ¼ tsp of pepper. Mix the ingredients.
5. Rinse and dry the fillet with a towel. Rub the fish with oil and sprinkle with pepper, paprika, and 2 Tbsp. of lemon.
6. Spread the spinach fillings on the fillets, then roll up each fillet ranging from the wide-angle and secure each fillet with toothpicks (use two.)
7. Bake for 15-20 minutes. Remove the toothpick and sprinkle with lemon peel.
8. Serve immediately.

Nutrition:
- Calories: 174kcal
- Carb: 1g
- Fat: 6g
- Protein 39g

46. Pickled Apple

Level of difficulty: Novice level
Preparation Time: 10 minutes
Cooking Time: 20 minutes
Servings: 6
Ingredients:

- Water (1/2 cup)
- Maple syrup (3 ½ oz.)
- Cider vinegar (1/2 cup)
- Sachet:
- Peppercorns (3-4)
- Mustard seed (1/4 tsp)
- Coriander seed (1/4 tsp)
- Salt (1/4 tsp)
- Granny smith apple (2,)
- Italian parsley (1 tbsp.,)

Directions:
1. Combine the water, maple syrup, vinegar, sachet, and sat in a saucepan. Bring to a boil.
2. Pour the liquid and the sachet over the apples in a nonreactive container.
3. Let it be refrigerated for 3-4 hours or overnight.
4. Drain the apples before serving and toss with the parsley.

Nutrition:
- 50 Calories
- 0.1g Fat
- 0.3g Protein

47. Baked Clams Oreganata

Level of difficulty: Intermediate
Preparation Time: 30 minutes
Cooking Time: 13 minutes
Servings: 10
Ingredients:

- Cherrystone clams (30)
- Olive oil (2 FL oz.)
- Onions (1 oz., chopped fine)
- Garlic (1 tsp, finely chopped)
- Lemon juice (1 FL oz.)
- Fresh breadcrumbs (10 oz.)
- Parsley (1 tbsp., chopped)
- Oregano (3/4 tsp, dried)
- White pepper (1/8 tsp)
- Parmesan cheese (1/3 cup)
- Paprika (as needed)
- Lemon wedges (10)

Directions:
1. Open the clams. Place the juice in a bowl.
2. Take out the clams from the shell. Situate them in a strainer over the bowl of juice. Let them drain 15 minutes in the refrigerator. Save the 30 best half-shells.
3. Cut the clams into small pieces.
4. Cook the oil in a sauté pan. Add the onion and garlic. Sauté about 1 minute, but do not brown.
5. Pour in half of the clam juice, then reduce it over high heat by three-fourths.
6. Remove from the heat and add the crumbs, parsley, lemon juice, white pepper, and oregano. Mix gently to avoid making the crumbs pasty.
7. If necessary, adjust the seasonings.
8. Once the mixture has cooled. Mix in the chopped clams.
9. Place the mixture in the 30 clamshells. Sprinkle with parmesan cheese and (very lightly) with paprika.
10. Place on a sheet pan and refrigerate until needed.
11. For each order, bake 3 clams in a hot oven (450 F) until they are hot and the top brown.
12. Garnish with a lemon wedge.

Nutrition:
- 180 Calories
- 8g Fat

- 10g Protein

48. Tuna Tartare

Level of difficulty: Novice level
Preparation Time: 15 minutes
Cooking Time: 0 minute
Servings: 8
Ingredients:
- Sashimi quality tuna (26.5 g, well-trimmed)
- Shallots (1 oz., minced)
- Parsley (2 tbsp., chopped)
- Fresh tarragon (2 tbsp., chopped)
- Lime juice (2 tbsp.)
- Dijon-style mustard (1 FL oz.)
- Olive oil (2 FL oz.)

Directions:
1. Use a knife to mince the tuna.
2. Mixed the rest of the ingredients with the chopped tuna.
3. Use a ring mold to make a beautifully presented tuna tartare.
4. Season to taste with pepper and salt.

Nutrition:
- 200 Calories
- 12g Fat
- 21g Protein

49. Cod Cakes

Level of difficulty: Novice level
Preparation Time: 25 minutes
Cooking Time: 30 minutes
Servings: 12
Ingredients:
- Cod (12 oz., cooked)
- Turnips puree (12 oz.)
- Whole eggs (2 ½ oz., beaten)
- Egg yolk (1 yolk, beaten)
- Salt (to taste)
- White pepper (to taste)
- Ground ginger (pinch)

Standard Breading Procedure:
- Whole wheat flour
- Egg wash
- Breadcrumbs
- Tomatoes sauce

Directions:
1. Shred the fish.
2. Combine with the turnips, egg, and egg yolk.
3. Season with salt, pepper, and ground ginger.
4. Divide the mixture into 2 ½ oz. portions. Shape the mixture into a ball and then slightly flatten the mixture cakes.
5. Place the mixture through the Standard Breading Procedure.
6. Deep-fry at 350 F until golden brown.
7. Serve 2 cakes per portion. Accompany with tomato sauce.

Nutrition:
- 280 Calories
- 6g Fat
- 23g Protein

50. Grilled Vegetable Kebabs

Level of difficulty: Novice level
Preparation Time: 12 minutes
Cooking Time: 13 minutes
Servings: 6
Ingredients:
- Zucchini (6 oz., trimmed)
- Yellow Summer Squash (6 oz., trimmed)
- Bell pepper (6 oz., red or orange, cut into 1 ½ in. squares)
- Onion (12 oz., red, large dice)
- Mushroom caps (12, medium)
- Olive oil (12 FL oz.)
- Garlic (1/2 oz., crushed)

- Rosemary (1 ½ tsp, dried)
- Thyme (1/2 tsp, dried)
- Salt (2 tsp)
- Black pepper (1/2 tsp)

Directions:
1. Cut the zucchini and yellow squash into 12 equal slices each.
2. Arrange the vegetables on 12 bamboo skewers. Give each skewer an equal arrangement of vegetable pieces.
3. Place the skewers in a single layer in a hotel pan.
4. Mix the oil, garlic, herbs, salt, and pepper to make a marinade.
5. Pour the marinade over the vegetables, turning them to coat completely.
6. Marinate 1 hour. Turn the skewers once or twice during margination to ensure the vegetables are coated.
7. Remove the skewers from the marinade and let the excess oil drip off.

Nutrition:
- 50 Calories
- 3g Fat
- 1g Protein

51. Manchego Crackers

Level of difficulty: Novice level
Preparation Time: 55 minutes
Cooking Time: 15 minutes
Servings: 4
Ingredients:
- 4 tbsp. butter, at room temperature
- 1 cup Manchego cheese
- 1 cup almond flour
- 1 teaspoon salt, divided
- ¼ teaspoon black pepper
- 1 large egg

Directions:
1. Using an electric mixer, scourge butter and shredded cheese.
2. Mix almond flour with ½ teaspoon salt and pepper. Mix almond flour mixture to the cheese, mixing constantly to form a ball.
3. Place onto plastic wrap and roll into a cylinder log about 1½ inches thick. Wrap tightly and cool for at least 1 hour.
4. Preheat the oven to 350°F. Prep two baking sheets with parchment papers.
5. For egg wash, blend egg and remaining ½ teaspoon salt.
6. Slice the refrigerated dough into small rounds, about ¼ inch thick, and place on the lined baking sheets.
7. Egg wash the tops of the crackers and bake for 15 minutes. Pull out from the oven and place in wire rack.
8. Serve.

Nutrition:
- 243 Calories
- 23g Fat
- 8g Protein

52. Burrata Caprese Stack

Level of difficulty: Novice level
Preparation Time: 5 minutes
Cooking Time: 0 minutes
Servings: 4
Ingredients:
- 1 large organic tomato
- ½ teaspoon salt
- ¼ teaspoon black pepper
- 1 (4-ounce) ball burrata cheese
- 8 fresh basil leaves
- 2 tbsp. extra-virgin olive oil
- 1 tbsp. red wine

Directions:
1. Slice the tomato into 4 thick slices, removing any tough center core and sprinkle with salt and pepper. Place the tomatoes, seasoned-side up, on a plate.

2. On a separate rimmed plate, slice the burrata into 4 thick slices and place one slice on top of each tomato slice. Top each with one-quarter of the basil and pour any reserved burrata cream from the rimmed plate over top.
3. Sprinkle with olive oil and vinegar.

Nutrition:
- 153 Calories
- 13g Fat
- 7g Protein

53. Zucchini-Ricotta Fritters with Lemon-Garlic Aioli

Level of difficulty: Novice level
Preparation Time: 30 minutes
Cooking Time: 25 minutes
Servings: 4
Ingredients:
- 1 large zucchini
- 1 teaspoon salt, divided
- ½ cup whole-milk ricotta cheese
- 2 scallions
- 1 large egg
- 2 garlic cloves
- 2 tbsp. fresh mint (optional)
- 2 teaspoons grated lemon zest
- ¼ teaspoon freshly ground black pepper
- ½ cup almond flour
- 1 teaspoon baking powder
- 8 tbsp. extra-virgin olive oil
- 8 tbsp. Roasted Garlic Aioli

Directions:
1. Place the shredded zucchini in a colander or on several layers of paper towels. Sprinkle with ½ teaspoon salt and let sit for 10 minutes. Using another layer of paper towel, press down on the zucchini to release any excess moisture and pat dry.
2. Incorporate drained zucchini, ricotta, scallions, egg, garlic, mint (if using), lemon zest, remaining ½ teaspoon salt, and pepper and stir well.
3. Blend almond flour and baking powder. Mix in flour mixture into the zucchini mixture and let rest for 10 minutes.
4. In a large skillet, working in four batches, fry the fritters. For each batch of four, heat 2 tbsp. olive oil over medium-high heat. Add 1 heaping tbsp. of zucchini batter per fritter, pressing down with the back of a spoon to form 2- to 3-inch fritters. Cover and let fry 2 minutes before flipping. Fry another 2 to 3 minutes, covered.
5. Repeat for the remaining three batches, using 2 tbsp. of the olive oil for each batch.
6. Serve with aioli.

Nutrition:
- 448 Calories
- 42g Fat
- 8g Protein

54. Salmon-Stuffed Cucumbers

Level of difficulty: Novice level
Preparation Time: 10 minutes
Cooking Time: 0 minute
Servings: 4
Ingredients:
- 2 large cucumbers, peeled
- 1 (4-ounce) can red salmon
- 1 medium very ripe avocado
- 1 tbsp. extra-virgin olive oil
- Zest and juice of 1 lime
- 3 tbsp. chopped fresh cilantro
- ½ teaspoon salt
- ¼ teaspoon black pepper

Directions:
1. Slice the cucumber into 1-inch-thick segments and using a spoon, scrape seeds out of center of each segment and stand up on a plate.
2. In a medium bowl, mix salmon, avocado, olive oil, lime zest and juice, cilantro, salt, and pepper.
3. Ladle the salmon mixture into the center of each cucumber segment and serve chilled.

Nutrition:
- 159 Calories
- 11g Fat
- 9g Protein

55. Goat Cheese–Mackerel Pâté

Level of difficulty: Novice level
Preparation Time: 10 minutes
Cooking Time: 0 minute
Servings: 4
Ingredients:
- 4 ounces olive oil-packed wild-caught mackerel
- 2 ounces goat cheese
- Zest and juice of 1 lemon
- 2 tbsp. chopped fresh parsley
- 2 tbsp. chopped fresh arugula
- 1 tbsp. extra-virgin olive oil
- 2 teaspoons chopped capers
- 2 teaspoons fresh horseradish (optional)

Directions:
1. In a food processor, blender, or large bowl with immersion blender, combine the mackerel, goat cheese, lemon zest and juice, parsley, arugula, olive oil, capers, and horseradish (if using). Process or blend until smooth and creamy.
2. Serve with crackers, cucumber rounds, endive spears, or celery.

Nutrition:
- 118 Calories
- 8g Fat
- 9g Protein

56. White Bean Dip with Garlic and Herbs

Level of difficulty: Novice level
Preparation Time: 10 minutes
Cooking Time: 48 minutes
Servings: 16
Ingredients:
- 1 cup dried white beans
- 3 cloves garlic
- 8 cups water
- ¼ cup extra-virgin olive oil
- ¼ cup chopped fresh flat-leaf parsley
- 1 tbsp. fresh oregano
- 1 tbsp. d fresh tarragon
- 1 teaspoon fresh thyme leaves
- 1 teaspoon lemon zest
- ¼ teaspoon salt
- ¼ teaspoon black pepper

Directions:
1. Place beans and garlic in the Instant Pot® and stir well. Add water, close lid, put steam release to Sealing, press the Manual, and adjust time to 30 minutes.
2. When the timer beeps, release naturally, about 20 minutes. Open and check if beans are soft. Press the Cancel button, drain off excess water, and transfer beans and garlic to a food processor with olive oil. Add parsley, oregano, tarragon, thyme, lemon zest, salt, and pepper, and pulse 3–5 times to mix. Chill for 4 hours or overnight. Serve cold or at room temperature.

Nutrition:

- 47 Calories
- 3g Fat
- 1g Protein

57. Black Bean Dip
Level of difficulty: Intermediate
Preparation Time: 14 minutes
Cooking Time: 53 minutes
Servings: 16
Ingredients:
- 1 tbsp. olive oil
- 2 slices bacon
- 1 small onion,
- 3 cloves garlic
- 1 cup low-sodium chicken broth
- 1 cup dried black beans
- 1 (14.5-ounce) can diced tomatoes
- 1 small jalapeño pepper
- 1 teaspoon ground cumin
- ½ teaspoon smoked paprika
- 1 tbsp. lime juice
- ½ teaspoon dried oregano
- ¼ cup minced fresh cilantro
- ¼ teaspoon sea salt

Directions:
1. Press the Sauté button on the Instant Pot® and heat oil. Add bacon and onion. Cook for 5 minutes. Cook garlic for 30 seconds. Fill in broth. Add beans, tomatoes, jalapeño, cumin, paprika, lime juice, oregano, cilantro, and salt. Press the Cancel button.
2. Close lid, let steam release to Sealing, set Bean button, and default time of 30 minutes. When the timer rings, let pressure release naturally for 10 minutes. Press the Cancel button and open lid.
3. Use an immersion blender blend the ingredients. Serve warm.

Nutrition:
- 60 Calories
- 2g Fat
- 3g Protein

58. Salsa Verde
Level of difficulty: Novice level
Preparation Time: 9 minutes
Cooking Time: 21 minutes
Servings: 8
Ingredients:
- 1-pound tomatillos
- 2 small jalapeño peppers
- 1 small onion
- ½ cup chopped fresh cilantro
- 1 teaspoon ground coriander
- 1 teaspoon sea salt
- 1½ cups water

Directions:
1. Cut tomatillos in half and place in the Instant Pot®. Add enough water to cover.
2. Close lids, set steam release to Sealing, press the Manual button, and set time to 2 minutes. Once timer beeps, release pressure naturally, for 20 minutes. Press the Cancel and open lid.
3. Drain off excess water and transfer tomatillos to a food processor or blender, and add jalapeños, onion, cilantro, coriander, salt, and water. Pulse until well combined, about 20 pulses.
4. Wrap and cool for 2 hours before serving.

Nutrition:
- 27 Calories
- 1g Fat
- 1g Protein

59. Greek Eggplant Dip

Level of difficulty: Novice level
Preparation Time: 16 minutes
Cooking Time: 3 minutes
Servings: 8
Ingredients:
- 1 cup water
- 1 large eggplant
- 1 clove garlic
- ½ teaspoon salt
- 1 tbsp. red wine vinegar
- ½ cup extra-virgin olive oil
- 2 tbsp. minced fresh parsley

Directions:
1. Add water to the Instant Pot®, add the rack to the pot, and place the steamer basket on the rack.
2. Place eggplant in steamer basket. Close, set steam release to Sealing, turn on Manual button, and set time to 3 minutes. When the timer stops, quick-release the pressure. Click Cancel button and open.
3. Situate eggplant to a food processor and add garlic, salt, and vinegar. Pulse until smooth, about 20 pulses.
4. Slowly add oil to the eggplant mixture while the food processor runs continuously until oil is completely incorporated. Stir in parsley. Serve at room temperature.

Nutrition:
- 134 Calories
- 14g Fat
- 1g Protein

60. Baba Ghanoush

Level of difficulty: Novice level
Preparation Time: 9 minutes
Cooking Time: 11 minutes
Servings: 8
Ingredients:
- 2 tbsp. extra-virgin olive oil
- 1 large eggplant
- 3 cloves garlic
- ½ cup water
- 3 tbsp. fresh flat-leaf parsley
- ½ teaspoon salt
- ¼ teaspoon smoked paprika
- 2 tbsp. lemon juice
- 2 tbsp. tahini

Directions:
1. Press the Sauté button on the Instant Pot® and add 1 tbsp. oil. Add eggplant and cook until it begins to soften, about 5 minutes. Add garlic and cook 30 seconds.
2. Add water and close lid, click steam release to Sealing, select Manual, and time to 6 minutes. Once the timer rings, quick-release the pressure. Select Cancel and open lid.
3. Strain cooked eggplant and garlic and add to a food processor or blender along with parsley, salt, smoked paprika, lemon juice, and tahini. Add remaining 1 tbsp. oil and process. Serve warm or at room temperature.

Nutrition:
- 79 Calories
- 6g Fat
- 2g Protein

61. Cheesy Caprese Salad Skewers

Level of difficulty: Novice level
Preparation Time: 15 minutes
Cooking Time: 0 minute
Servings: 10
Ingredients:
- 8-oz cherry tomatoes, sliced in half

- A handful of fresh basil leaves, rinsed and drained
- 1-lb fresh mozzarella, cut into bite-sized slices
- Balsamic vinegar
- Extra virgin olive oil
- Freshly ground black pepper

Directions:
1. Sandwich a folded basil leaf and mozzarella cheese between the halves of tomato onto a toothpick.
2. Drizzle with olive oil and balsamic vinegar each skewer. To serve, sprinkle with freshly ground black pepper.

Nutrition:
- 94 Calories
- 3.7g Fats
- 2.1g Protein

62. Leafy Lacinato Tuscan Treat

Level of difficulty: Novice level
Preparation Time: 10 minutes
Cooking Time: 0 minute
Servings: 1
Ingredients:
- 1-tsp Dijon mustard
- 1-tbsp light mayonnaise
- 3-pcs medium-sized Lacinato kale leaves
- 3-oz. cooked chicken breast, thinly sliced
- 6-bulbs red onion, thinly sliced
- 1-pc apple, cut into 9-slices

Directions:
1. Mix the mustard and mayonnaise until fully combined.
2. Spread the mixture generously on each of the kale leaves. Top each leaf with 1-oz. chicken slices, 3-apple slices, and 2-red onion slices. Roll each kale leaf into a wrap.

Nutrition:
- 370 Calories
- 14g Fats
- 29g Protein

63. Greek Guacamole Hybrid Hummus

Level of difficulty: Intermediate
Preparation Time: 10 minutes
Cooking Time: 0 minute
Servings: 1
Ingredients:
- 1-15 oz. canned chickpeas
- 1-pc ripe avocado
- ¼-cup tahini paste
- 1-cup fresh cilantro leaves
- ¼-cup lemon juice
- 1-tsp ground cumin
- ¼-cup extra-virgin olive oil
- 1-clove garlic
- ½ tsp salt

Directions:
1. Drain the chickpeas and reserve 2-tbsp. of the liquid. Pour the reserved liquid in your food processor and add in the drained chickpeas.
2. Add the avocado, tahini, cilantro, lemon juice, cumin, oil, garlic, and salt. Puree the mixture into a smooth consistency.
3. Serve with pita chips, veggie chips, or crudités.

Nutrition:
- 156 Calories
- 12g Fats
- 3g Protein

64. Packed Picnic

Level of difficulty: Novice level
Preparation Time: 5 minutes
Cooking Time: 0 minute

Servings: 1
Ingredients:
- 1-slice of whole-wheat bread, cut into bite-size pieces
- 10-pcs cherry tomatoes
- ¼-oz. aged cheese, sliced
- 6-pcs oil-cured olives

Directions:
1. Pack each of the ingredients in a portable container to serve you while snacking on the go.

Nutrition:
- 197 Calories
- 9g Fats
- 7g Protein

65. Pizza & Pastry

Level of difficulty: Novice level
Preparation Time: 35 minutes
Cooking Time: 15 minutes
Servings: 10
Ingredients:

For Pizza Dough:
- 2-tsp honey
- ¼-oz. active dry yeast
- 1¼-cups warm water (about 120 °F)
- 2-tbsp olive oil
- 1-tsp sea salt
- 3-cups whole grain flour + ¼-cup, as needed for rolling

For Pizza Topping:
- 1-cup pesto sauce (refer to Perky Pesto recipe)
- 1-cup artichoke hearts
- 1-cup wilted spinach leaves
- 1-cup sun-dried tomato
- ½-cup Kalamata olives
- 4-oz. feta cheese
- 4-oz. mixed cheese of equal parts low-fat mozzarella, asiago, and provolone

Optional:
- Bell pepper
- Chicken breast, strips
- Fresh basil
- Pine nuts

Directions:
For the Pizza Dough:
1. Preheat your oven to 350 °F.
2. Combine the honey and yeast with the warm water in your food processor with a dough attachment. Blend the mixture until fully combined. Set aside the mixture for 5 minutes to ensure the activity of the yeast through the appearance of bubbles on the surface.
3. Pour in the olive oil. Add the salt, and blend for half a minute. Add gradually 3 cups of flour, about half a cup at a time, blending for a couple of minutes between each addition.
4. Let your processor knead the mixture for 10 minutes until smooth and elastic, sprinkling it with flour whenever necessary to prevent the dough from sticking to the processor bowl's surfaces.
5. Take the dough from the bowl. Let it stand for 15 minutes, covered with a moist, warm towel.
6. Using a rolling pin, roll out the dough to a half-inch thickness, dusting it with flour as needed. Poke holes indiscriminately on the dough using a fork to prevent crust bubbling.
7. Place the perforated, rolled dough on a pizza stone or baking sheet. Bake for 5 minutes.

For Pizza Topping:
8. Lightly brush the baked pizza shell with olive oil.
9. Pour over the pesto sauce and spread thoroughly over the pizza shell's surface, leaving out a half-inch space around its edge as the crust.
10. Top the pizza with artichoke hearts, wilted spinach leaves, sun-dried tomatoes, and olives. Cover the top with the cheese.

11. Situate pizza directly on the oven rack. Bake for 10 minutes. Set aside for 5 minutes before slicing.

Nutrition:
- 242.8 Calories
- 15g Fats
- 14g Protein

66. Cashews and Red Cabbage Salad

Level of difficulty: Novice level
Preparation Time: 10 minutes
Cooking Time: 0 minutes
Servings: 4
Ingredients:
- 1-pound red cabbage, shredded
- 2 tbsp. coriander, chopped
- ½ cup cashews halved
- 2 tbsp. olive oil
- 1 tomato, cubed
- A pinch of salt and black pepper
- 1 tbsp. white vinegar

Directions:
1. Mix the cabbage with the coriander and the rest of the ingredients in a salad bowl, toss and serve cold.

Nutrition:
- 210 Calories
- 6.3g Fat
- 8g Protein

67. Apples and Pomegranate Salad

Level of difficulty: Novice level
Preparation Time: 10 minutes
Cooking Time: 0 minutes
Servings: 4
Ingredients:
- 3 big apples, cored and cubed
- 1 cup pomegranate seeds
- 3 cups baby arugula
- 1 cup walnuts, chopped
- 1 tbsp. olive oil
- 1 teaspoon white sesame seeds
- 2 tbsp. apple cider vinegar

Directions:
1. Mix the apples with the arugula and the rest of the ingredients in a bowl, toss and serve cold.

Nutrition:
- 160 Calories
- 4.3g Fat
- 10g Protein

68. Cranberry Bulgur Mix

Level of difficulty: Novice level
Preparation Time: 10 minutes
Cooking Time: 0 minutes
Servings: 4
Ingredients:
- 1 and ½ cups hot water
- 1 cup bulgur
- Juice of ½ lemon
- 4 tbsp. cilantro, chopped
- ½ cup cranberries
- 1 and ½ teaspoons curry powder
- ¼ cup green onions
- ½ cup red bell peppers
- ½ cup carrots, grated
- 1 tbsp. olive oil

Directions:
1. Put bulgur into a bowl, add the water, stir, cover, leave aside for 10 minutes, fluff with a fork, and situate to a bowl. Add the rest of the ingredients, toss, and serve cold.

Nutrition:
- 300 Calories
- 6.4g Fat
- 13g Protein

69. Chickpeas, Corn and Black Beans Salad

Level of difficulty: Intermediate
Preparation Time: 10 minutes
Cooking Time: 0 minutes
Servings: 4
Ingredients:
- 1 and ½ cups canned black beans
- ½ teaspoon garlic powder
- 2 teaspoons chili powder
- 1 and ½ cups canned chickpeas
- 1 cup baby spinach
- 1 avocado, pitted, peeled, and chopped
- 1 cup corn kernels, chopped
- 2 tbsp. lemon juice
- 1 tbsp. olive oil
- 1 tbsp. apple cider vinegar
- 1 teaspoon chives, chopped

Directions:
1. Mix the black beans with the garlic powder, chili powder, and the rest of the ingredients in a bowl, toss and serve cold.

Nutrition:
- 300 Calories
- 13.4g Fat
- 13g Protein

70. Olives and Lentils Salad

Level of difficulty: Novice level
Preparation Time: 10 minutes
Cooking Time: 0 minutes
Servings: 2
Ingredients:
- 1/3 cup canned green lentils
- 1 tbsp. olive oil
- 2 cups baby spinach
- 1 cup black olives
- 2 tbsp. sunflower seeds
- 1 tbsp. Dijon mustard
- 2 tbsp. balsamic vinegar
- 2 tbsp. olive oil

Directions:
1. Mix the lentils with the spinach, olives, and the rest of the ingredients in a salad bowl, toss and serve cold.

Nutrition:
- 279 Calories
- 6.5g Fat
- 12g Protein

71. Lime Spinach and Chickpeas Salad

Level of difficulty: Novice level
Preparation Time: 10 minutes
Cooking Time: 0 minutes
Servings: 4
Ingredients:
- 16 ounces canned chickpeas
- 2 cups baby spinach leaves
- ½ tbsp. lime juice
- 2 tbsp. olive oil
- 1 teaspoon cumin, ground
- ½ teaspoon chili flakes

Directions:
1. Mix the chickpeas with the spinach and the rest of the ingredients in a large bowl, toss and serve cold.

Nutrition:
- 240 calories
- 8.2g fat
- 12g protein

72. Minty Olives and Tomatoes Salad

Level of difficulty: Novice level
Preparation Time: 10 minutes
Cooking Time: 0 minutes
Servings: 4
Ingredients:
- 1 cup kalamata olives

- 1 cup black olives
- 1 cup cherry tomatoes
- 4 tomatoes
- 1 red onion, chopped
- 2 tbsp. oregano, chopped
- 1 tbsp. mint, chopped
- 2 tbsp. balsamic vinegar
- ¼ cup olive oil
- 2 teaspoons Italian herbs, dried

Directions:
1. In a salad bowl, mix the olives with the tomatoes and the rest of the ingredients, toss, and serve cold.

Nutrition:
- 190 Calories
- 8.1g Fat
- 4.6g Protein

73. Roasted Beet Salad with Ricotta Cheese

Level of difficulty: Novice level
Preparation Time: 10 minutes
Cooking Time: 1 hour
Servings: 4
Ingredients:
- Red beets (8.8 oz., large, wrapped in foil)
- Yellow beets (8.8 oz., small, wrapped in foil)
- Mesclun (4.3 oz.)
- Mustard Vinaigrette (4.4 oz.)
- Ricotta cheese (2.1 oz.)
- Walnuts (0.1 oz., chopped)

Directions:
1. Bake at 400 F for 1 hour.
2. Set aside the beets lightly. Cut the root and stem ends and pull off the peels.
3. Chop the red beets crosswise into thin slices.
4. Cut the yellow beets vertically into quarters.
5. Arrange the sliced red beets in circles on cold salad plates. Toss the mesclun with half the vinaigrette.
6. Pour in the remaining vinaigrette over the sliced beets.
7. Place small mound of greens in the center of each plate.
8. Lay out the quartered yellow beets around the greens.
9. Drizzle the tops with the crumbled ricotta and walnuts (if using).

Nutrition:
- 290 Calories
- 6g Fat
- 6g Protein

74. Baked Fish with Tomatoes and Mushrooms

Level of difficulty: Intermediate
Preparation Time: 12 minutes
Cooking Time: 25 minutes
Servings: 4
Ingredients:
- Fish (4, whole and small, 12 oz. each)
- Salt (to taste)
- Pepper (to taste)
- Dried thyme (pinch)
- Parsley (4 sprigs)
- Olive oil (as needed)
- Onion (4 oz., small dice)
- Shallots (1 oz., minced)
- Mushrooms (8 oz., chopped)
- Tomato concassed (6.4 oz.)
- Dry white wine (3.2 FL oz.)

Directions:
1. Scale and clean the fish but leaves the heads on. Season the fish inside and out with salt and pepper and put a small pinch of thyme and a sprig of parsley in the cavity of each.

2. Use as many baking pans to hold the fish in a single layer. Oil the pans with a little olive oil.
3. Sauté the onions and shallots in a little olive oil about 1 minute. Add the mushrooms and sauté lightly.
4. Place the sautéed vegetables and the tomatoes in the bottoms of the baking pans.
5. Place the fish in the pans. Oil the tops lightly. Pour in the wine.
6. Bake at 400F for 15-20 minutes.
7. Remove the fish and keep them warm.
8. Remove the vegetables from the pans with a slotted spoon and check for seasonings. Serve a spoonful of the vegetables with the fish, placing it under or alongside each fish.
9. Strain, degrease, and reduce the cooking liquid slightly. Just before serving, moisten each portion with 1-2 tbsp. of the liquid.

Nutrition:
- 350 Calories
- 9g Fat
- 55g Protein

75. Goat Cheese and Walnut Salad

Level of difficulty: Novice level
Preparation Time: 15 minutes
Cooking Time: 10 minutes
Servings: 3
Ingredients:
- Beet (2 oz.)
- Arugula (3 oz.)
- Bibb lettuce (2 oz.)
- Romaine lettuce (9 oz.)
- Breadcrumbs (1/4 cup, dry)
- Dried thyme (1/4 tbsp.)
- Dried basil (1/4 tbsp.)
- Black pepper (1/3 tsp)
- Fresh goat's milk cheese (6.35 oz., preferably in log shape)
- Walnut pieces (1.1 oz.)
- Red wine vinaigrette (2 fl. Oz.)

Directions:
1. Trim, wash, and dry all the salad greens.
2. Tear the greens into small pieces. Toss well.
3. Combine the herbs, pepper, and crumbs.
4. Slice the cheese into 1 oz. pieces. In the seasoned crumbs mix, roll the pieces of cheese to coat them
5. Place the cheese on a sheet pan. Bake at the temperate of 425 F for 10 minutes.
6. Simultaneously, toast the walnuts in a dry sauté pan or the oven with the cheese.
7. Toss the greens with the vinaigrette and arrange on cold plates. Top each plate of greens with 2 pieces of cheese and sprinkle with walnuts.

Nutrition:
- 460 Calories
- 40g Fat
- 17g Protein

76. Grilled Spiced Turkey Burger

Level of difficulty: Intermediate
Preparation Time: 15 minutes
Cooking Time: 20 minutes
Servings: 3
Ingredients:
- Onion (1.8 oz., chopped fine)
- Extra Virgin Olive Oil (1/3 tbsp.)
- Turkey (14.4 oz., ground)
- Salt (1/3 tbsp.)
- Curry powder (1/3 tbsp.)

- Lemon zest (2/5 tsp, grated)
- Pepper (1/8 tsp)
- Cinnamon (1/8 tsp)
- Coriander (1/4 tsp, ground)
- Cumin (1/8 tsp, ground)
- Cardamom (1/8 tsp, ground)
- Water (1.2 FL oz.)
- Tomato Raisin Chutney (as desired)
- Cilantro leaves (as desired)

Directions:
1. Cook the onions in the oil. Cool completely.
2. Combine the turkey, onions, spices, water, and salt in a bowl. Toss.
3. Divide the mixture into 5 oz. portions (or as desired). Form each portion into a thick patty.
4. Broil but do not overcook it.
5. Plate the burgers. Put spoonful of chutney on top of each.

Nutrition:
- 250 Calories
- 14g Fat
- 27g Protein

77. Tomato Tea Party Sandwiches

Level of difficulty: Novice level
Preparation Time: 15 minutes
Cooking Time: 0 minute
Servings: 4
Ingredients:
- Whole wheat bread (4 slices)
- Extra virgin olive oil (4 1/3 tbsp.)
- Basil (2 1/8 tbsp., minced)
- Tomato slices (4 thick)
- Ricotta cheese (4 oz.)
- Dash of pepper

Directions:
1. Toast bread to your preference.
2. Spread 2 tsp. olive oil on each slice of bread. Add the cheese.
3. Top with tomato, then sprinkle with basil and pepper.
4. Serve with lemon water and enjoy it!

Nutrition:
- 239 Calories
- 16.4g Fat
- 6g Protein

78. Veggie Shish Kebabs

Level of difficulty: Novice level
Preparation Time: 10 minutes
Cooking Time: 0 minute
Servings: 3
Ingredients:
- Cherry tomatoes (9)
- Mozzarella balls (9 low-fat)
- Basil leaves (9)
- Olive oil (1 tsp.)
- Zucchini (3, sliced)
- Dash of pepper

For Servings:
- Whole Wheat Bread (6 slices)

Directions:
1. Stab 1 cherry tomato, low-fat mozzarella ball, zucchini, and basil leaf onto each skewer.
2. Place skewers on a plate and drizzle with olive oil. Finish with a sprinkle of pepper.
3. Set your bread to toast. Serve 2 bread slices with 3 kebobs.

Nutrition:
- 349 Calories
- 5.7g Fat
- 15g Protein

79. Crispy Falafel

Level of difficulty: Novice level
Preparation Time: 20 minutes
Cooking Time: 8 minutes
Servings: 3
Ingredients:
- Chickpeas (1 cup, drained and rinsed)
- Parsley (½ cup, chopped with stems removed)
- Cilantro (1/3 cup, chopped with stems removed)
- Dill (¼ cup, chopped with stems removed)
- Cloves garlic (4, minced)
- Sesame seeds (1 tbsp., toasted)
- Coriander (½ tbsp.)
- Black pepper (½ tbsp.)
- Cumin (½ tbsp.)
- Baking powder (½ tsp.)
- Cayenne (½ tsp.)

Directions:
1. Thoroughly dry your chickpeas with a paper towel.
2. Place the parsley, cilantro, and dill in a food processor.
3. Mix chickpeas, garlic, coriander, black pepper, cumin, baking powder, and cayenne.
4. Place the mixture to an airtight container and chill for about an hour.
5. Take out from the refrigerator and mix the baking powder and sesame seeds.
6. Scoop the mixture into a pan with 3 inches of olive oil over medium heat to create patties. Keep in mind as you create the patties that you are aiming to make 12 with the mixture.
7. Let the falafel patties fry for 1-2 minutes on each side.
8. Once your falafel patties are nicely browned, transfer them to a plate lined with paper towels to finish crisping.
9. Dip, dunk, fill, and enjoy!

Nutrition:
- 328 Calories
- 10.8g Fat
- 24g Protein

80. Onion Fried Eggs

Level of difficulty: Novice level
Preparation Time: 15 minutes
Cooking Time: 91 minutes
Servings: 4
Ingredients:
- Eggs (11)
- White mushroom (1 cup)
- Feta cheese (4 oz., crumbled)
- Sun-dried tomatoes (1/2 cup, chopped)
- Onion (2 larges, sliced)
- Garlic clove (2, minced)
- Olive oil (2.5 tbsp.)

Directions:
1. Place a pan with the olive oil over medium-low heat.
2. Once hot, stir onions and mushrooms into the oil.
3. Allow the onion and mushroom mix to cook for about one hour. Stir them every 5-7 minutes to ensure they cook evenly.
4. After the onions have browned, add the sun-dried tomatoes and garlic, and let cook for 2 minutes.
5. Once the sun-dried tomatoes and garlic are fragrant, spread all the ingredients out into an even, thin layer across the pan.
6. Crack the eggs overtop the ingredients already in the pan.
7. Sprinkle your feta cheese and pepper over top of the eggs.
8. Cover the pan with its corresponding lid and let the eggs sit to cook for about

10-12 minutes. Gently shake the pan at 10 minutes to check on the consistency of the egg yolks. Continue cooking until desired level of doneness.
9. Remove pan from heat and divide the mixture between two plates.

Nutrition:
- 360 Calories
- 27g Fat
- 20g Protein

CHAPTER 4. DINNER

81. Savoy Cabbage with Coconut Cream Sauce

Level of difficulty: Intermediate
Preparation Time: 5 minutes
Cooking Time: 20 minute
Servings: 4
Ingredients:
- 3 tbsp. olive oil
- 1 onion, chopped
- 4 cloves of garlic, minced
- 1 head savoy cabbage, chopped finely
- 2 cups bone broth
- 1 cup coconut milk, freshly squeezed
- 1 bay leaf
- Salt and pepper to taste
- 2 tbsp. chopped parsley

Directions:
1. Heat oil in a pot for 2 minutes.
2. Stir in the onions, bay leaf, and garlic until fragrant, around 3 minutes.
3. Add the rest of the ingredients, except for the parsley and mix well.
4. Cover pot, bring to a boil, and let it simmer for 5 minutes or until cabbage is tender to taste.
5. Stir in parsley and serve.

Nutrition:
- Calories: 195;
- Carbs: 12.3g;
- Protein: 2.7g;
- Fat: 19.7g

82. Slow Cooked Buttery Mushrooms

Level of difficulty: Novice level
Preparation Time: 10 minutes
Cooking Time: 10 minute
Servings: 2
Ingredients:
- 2 tbsp. butter
- 2 tbsp. olive oil
- 3 cloves of garlic, minced
- 16 ounces fresh brown mushrooms, sliced
- 7 ounces fresh shiitake mushrooms, sliced
- A dash of thyme
- Salt and pepper to taste

Directions:
1. Heat the butter and oil in a pot.
2. Sauté the garlic until fragrant, around 1 minute.
3. Stir in the rest of the ingredients and cook until soft, around 9 minutes.

Nutrition:
- Calories: 192;
- Carbs: 12.7g;
- Protein: 3.8g;
- Fat: 15.5g

83. Steamed Squash Chowder

Level of difficulty: Novice level
Preparation Time: 20 minutes
Cooking Time: 40 minute
Servings: 4
Ingredients:
- 3 cups chicken broth
- 2 tbsp. ghee
- 1 teaspoon chili powder
- ½ teaspoon cumin
- 1 ½ teaspoon salt
- 2 teaspoon cinnamon
- 3 tbsp. olive oil
- 2 carrots, chopped
- 1 small yellow onion, chopped

- 1 green apple, sliced and cored
- 1 large butternut squash, peeled, seeded, and chopped to ½-inch cubes

Directions:
1. In a large pot on medium high fire, melt ghee.
2. Once ghee is hot, sauté onions for 5 minutes or until soft and translucent.
3. Add olive oil, chili powder, cumin, salt, and cinnamon. Sauté for half a minute.
4. Add chopped squash and apples.
5. Sauté for 10 minutes while stirring once in a while.
6. Add broth, cover and cook on medium fire for twenty minutes or until apples and squash are tender.
7. With an immersion blender, puree chowder. Adjust consistency by adding more water.
8. Add more salt or pepper depending on desire.
9. Serve and enjoy.

Nutrition:
- Calories: 228;
- Carbs: 17.9g;
- Protein: 2.2g;
- Fat: 18.0g

84. Steamed Zucchini-Paprika

Level of difficulty: Novice level
Preparation Time: 15 minutes
Cooking Time: 30 minute
Servings: 2
Ingredients:
- 4 tbsp. olive oil
- 3 cloves of garlic, minced
- 1 onion, chopped
- 3 medium-sized zucchinis, sliced thinly
- A dash of paprika
- Salt and pepper to taste

Directions:
1. Place all ingredients in the Instant Pot.
2. Give a good stir to combine all ingredients.
3. Close the lid and make sure that the steam release valve is set to "Venting."
4. Press the "Slow Cook" button and adjust the cooking time to 4 hours.
5. Halfway through the cooking time, open the lid and give a good stir to brown the other side.

Nutrition:
- Calories: 93;
- Carbs: 3.1g;
- Protein: 0.6g;
- Fat: 10.2g

85. Stir Fried Brussels sprouts and Carrots

Level of difficulty: Novice level
Preparation Time: 10 minutes
Cooking Time: 15 minute
Servings: 6
Ingredients:
- 1 tbsp. cider vinegar
- 1/3 cup water
- 1 lb. Brussels sprouts, halved lengthwise
- 1 lb. carrots cut diagonally into ½-inch thick lengths
- 3 tbsp. unsalted butter, divided
- 2 tbsp. chopped shallot
- ½ teaspoon pepper
- ¾ teaspoon salt

Directions:
1. On medium high fire, place a nonstick medium fry pan and heat 2 tbsp. butter.

2. Add shallots and cook until softened, around one to two minutes while occasionally stirring.
3. Add pepper salt, Brussels sprouts and carrots. Stir fry until vegetables starts to brown on the edges, around 3 to 4 minutes.
4. Add water, cook and cover.
5. After 5 to 8 minutes, or when veggies are already soft, add remaining butter.
6. If needed season with more pepper and salt to taste.
7. Turn off fire, transfer to a platter, serve and enjoy.

Nutrition:
- Calories: 98;
- Carbs: 13.9g;
- Protein: 3.5g;
- Fat: 4.2g

86. Stir Fried Eggplant

Level of difficulty: Novice level
Preparation Time: 10 minutes
Cooking Time: 30 minute
Servings: 2
Ingredients:
- 1 teaspoon cornstarch + 2 tbsp. water, mixed
- 1 teaspoon brown sugar
- 2 tbsp. oyster sauce
- 1 tbsp. fish sauce
- 2 tbsp. soy sauce
- ½ cup fresh basil
- 2 tbsp. oil
- ¼ cup water
- 2 cups Chinese eggplant, spiral
- 1 red chili
- 6 cloves garlic, minced
- ½ purple onion, sliced thinly
- 1 3-oz package medium firm tofu, cut into slivers

Directions:
1. Prepare sauce by mixing cornstarch and water in a small bowl. In another bowl mix brown sugar, oyster sauce and fish sauce and set aside.
2. On medium high fire, place a large nonstick saucepan and heat 2 tbsp. oil. Sauté chili, garlic and onion for 4 minutes. Add tofu, stir fry for 4 minutes.
3. Add eggplant noodles and stir fry for 10 minutes. If pan dries up, add water in small amounts to moisten pan and cook noodles.
4. Pour in sauce and mix well. Once simmering, slowly add cornstarch mixer while continuing to mix vigorously. Once sauce thickens add fresh basil and cook for a minute.
5. Remove from fire, transfer to a serving plate and enjoy.

Nutrition:
- Calories: 369;
- Carbs: 28.4g;
- Protein: 11.4g;
- Fat: 25.3g

87. Summer Vegetables

Level of difficulty: Novice level
Preparation Time: 20 minutes
Cooking Time: 1 hour 40 minutes minute
Servings: 6
Ingredients:
- 1 teaspoon dried marjoram
- 1/3 cup Parmesan cheese
- 1 small eggplant, sliced into ¼-inch thick circles
- 1 small summer squash, peeled and sliced diagonally into ¼-inch thickness
- 3 large tomatoes, sliced into ¼-inch thick circles
- ½ cup dry white wine

- ½ teaspoon freshly ground pepper, divided
- ½ teaspoon salt, divided
- 5 cloves garlic, sliced thinly
- 2 cups leeks, sliced thinly
- 4 tbsp. extra-virgin olive oil, divided

Directions:
1. On medium fire, place a large nonstick saucepan and heat 2 tbsp. oil.
2. Sauté garlic and leeks for 6 minutes or until garlic is starting to brown. Season with pepper and salt, ¼ teaspoon each.
3. Pour in wine and cook for another minute. Transfer to a 2-quart baking dish.
4. In baking dish, layer in alternating pattern the eggplant, summer squash, and tomatoes. Do this until dish is covered with vegetables. If there are excess vegetables, store for future use.
5. Season with remaining pepper and salt. Drizzle with remaining olive oil and pop in a preheated 425oF oven.
6. Bake for 75 minutes. Remove from oven and top with marjoram and cheese.
7. Return to oven and bake for 15 minutes more or until veggies are soft and edges are browned.
8. Allow to cool for at least 5 minutes before serving.

Nutrition:
- Calories: 150;
- Carbs: 11.8g;
- Protein: 3.3g;
- Fat: 10.8g

Vegetarian dishes

88. Stir Fried Bok Choy

Level of difficulty: Intermediate
Preparation Time: 5 minutes
Cooking Time: 13 minute
Servings: 4
Ingredients:
- 3 tbsp. coconut oil
- 4 cloves of garlic, minced
- 1 onion, chopped
- 2 heads bok choy, rinsed and chopped
- 2 teaspoons coconut aminos
- Salt and pepper to taste
- 2 tbsp. sesame oil
- 2 tbsp. sesame seeds, toasted

Directions:
1. Heat the oil in a pot for 2 minutes.
2. Sauté the garlic and onions until fragrant, around 3 minutes.
3. Stir in the bok choy, coconut aminos, salt and pepper.
4. Cover pan and cook for 5 minutes.
5. Stir and continue cooking for another 3 minutes.
6. Drizzle with sesame oil and sesame seeds on top before serving.

Nutrition:
- Calories: 358;
- Carbs: 5.2g;
- Protein: 21.5g;
- Fat: 28.4g

89. Summer Veggies in Instant Pot

Level of difficulty: Novice level
Preparation Time: 10 minutes
Cooking Time: 7 minute
Servings: 6
Ingredients:
- 2 cups okra, sliced
- 1 cup grape tomatoes
- 1 cup mushroom, sliced
- 1 ½ cups onion, sliced
- 2 cups bell pepper, sliced

- 2 ½ cups zucchini, sliced
- 2 tbsp. basil, chopped
- 1 tbsp. thyme, chopped
- ½ cups balsamic vinegar
- ½ cups olive oil
- Salt and pepper

Directions:
1. Place all ingredients in the Instant Pot.
2. Stir the contents and close the lid.
3. Close the lid and press the Manual button.
4. Adjust the cooking time to 7 minutes.
5. Do quick pressure release.
6. Once cooled, evenly divide into serving size, keep in your preferred container, and refrigerate until ready to eat.

Nutrition:
- Calories per Servings: 233;
- Carbs: 7g;
- Protein: 3g;
- Fat: 18g

90. Sumptuous Tomato Soup

Level of difficulty: Novice level
Preparation Time: 10 minutes
Cooking Time: 30 minute
Servings: 2
Ingredients:
- Pepper and salt to taste
- 2 tbsp. tomato paste
- 1 ½ cups vegetable broth
- 1 tbsp. chopped parsley
- 1 tbsp. olive oil
- 5 garlic cloves
- ½ medium yellow onion
- 4 large ripe tomatoes

Directions:
1. Preheat oven to 350oF.
2. Chop onion and tomatoes into thin wedges. Place on a rimmed baking sheet. Season with parsley, pepper, salt, and olive oil. Toss to combine well. Hide the garlic cloves inside tomatoes to keep it from burning.
3. Pop in the oven and bake for 30 minutes.
4. On medium pot, bring vegetable stock to a simmer. Add tomato paste.
5. Pour baked tomato mixture into pot. Continue simmering for another 10 minutes.
6. With an immersion blender, puree soup.
7. Adjust salt and pepper to taste before serving.

Nutrition:
- Calories: 179;
- Carbs: 26.7g;
- Protein: 5.2g;
- Fat: 7.7g

91. Avocado Peach Salsa on Grilled Swordfish

Level of difficulty: Novice level
Preparation Time: 15 minutes
Cooking Time: 12 minutes
Servings: 2
Ingredients:
- 1 garlic clove, minced
- 1 lemon juice
- 1 tbsp. apple cider vinegar
- 1 tbsp. coconut oil
- 1 teaspoon honey
- 2 swordfish fillets (around 4oz each)
- Pinch cayenne pepper
- Pinch of pepper and salt

Salsa Ingredients:
- ¼ red onion, finely chopped
- ½ cup cilantro, finely chopped

- 1 avocado, halved and diced
- 1 garlic clove, minced
- 2 peaches, seeded and diced
- Juice of 1 lime
- Salt to taste

Directions:
1. In a shallow dish, mix all swordfish marinade ingredients except fillet. Mix well then add fillets to marinate. Place in refrigerator for at least an hour.
2. Meanwhile create salsa by mixing all salsa ingredients in a medium bowl. Put in the refrigerator to cool.
3. Preheat grill and grill fish on medium fire after marinating until cooked around 4 minutes per side.
4. Place each cooked fillet on one serving plate, top with half of salsa, serve and enjoy.

Nutrition:
- Calories: 416;
- Carbohydrates: 21g;
- Protein: 30g;
- Fat: 23.5g

92. Breaded and Spiced Halibut

Level of difficulty: Novice level
Preparation Time: 10 minutes
Cooking Time: 15 minutes
Servings: 4
Ingredients:
- ¼ cup chopped fresh chives
- ¼ cup chopped fresh dill
- ¼ teaspoon ground black pepper
- ¾ cup panko breadcrumbs
- 1 tbsp. extra-virgin olive oil
- 1 teaspoon finely grated lemon zest
- 1 teaspoon sea salt
- 1/3 cup chopped fresh parsley
- 4 pieces of 6-oz halibut fillets

Directions:
1. Line a baking sheet with foil, grease with cooking spray and preheat oven to 400oF.
2. In a small bowl, mix black pepper, sea salt, lemon zest, olive oil, chives, dill, parsley and breadcrumbs. If needed add more salt to taste. Set aside.
3. Meanwhile, wash halibut fillets on cold tap water. Dry with paper towels and place on prepared baking sheet.
4. Generously spoon crumb mixture onto halibut fillets. Ensure that fillets are covered with crumb mixture. Press down on crumb mixture onto each fillet.
5. Pop into the oven and bake for 10-15 minutes or until fish is flaky and crumb topping are already lightly browned.

Nutrition:
- Calories: 336.4;
- Protein: 25.3g;
- Fat: 25.3g;
- Carbs: 4.1g

93. Berries and Grilled Calamari

Level of difficulty: Novice level
Preparation Time: 10 minutes
Cooking Time: 5 minutes
Servings: 4
Ingredients:
- ¼ cup dried cranberries
- ¼ cup extra virgin olive oil
- ¼ cup olive oil
- ¼ cup sliced almonds
- ½ lemon, juiced
- ¾ cup blueberries
- 1 ½ pounds calamari tube, cleaned
- 1 granny smith apple, sliced thinly

- 1 tbsp. fresh lemon juice
- 2 tbsp. apple cider vinegar
- 6 cups fresh spinach
- Freshly grated pepper to taste
- Sea salt to taste

Directions:
1. In a small bowl, make the vinaigrette by mixing well the tbsp. of lemon juice, apple cider vinegar, and extra virgin olive oil. Season with pepper and salt to taste. Set aside.
2. Turn on the grill to medium fire and let the grates heat up for a minute or two.
3. In a large bowl, add olive oil and the calamari tube. Season calamari generously with pepper and salt.
4. Place seasoned and oiled calamari onto heated grate and grill until cooked or opaque. This is around two minutes per side.
5. As you wait for the calamari to cook, you can combine almonds, cranberries, blueberries, spinach, and the thinly sliced apple in a large salad bowl. Toss to mix.
6. Remove cooked calamari from grill and transfer on a chopping board. Cut into ¼-inch thick rings and throw into the salad bowl.
7. Drizzle with vinaigrette and toss well to coat salad.

Serve and enjoy!

Nutrition:
- Calories: 567;
- Fat: 24.5g;
- Protein: 54.8g;
- Carbs: 30.6g
- Fish and Seafood

94. Coconut Salsa on Chipotle Fish Tacos

Level of difficulty: Novice level

Preparation Time: 10 minutes
Cooking Time: 10 minutes
Servings: 4

Ingredients:
- ¼ cup chopped fresh cilantro
- ½ cup seeded and finely chopped plum tomato
- 1 cup peeled and finely chopped mango
- 1 lime cut into wedges
- 1 tbsp. chipotle Chile powder
- 1 tbsp. safflower oil
- 1/3 cup finely chopped red onion
- 10 tbsp. fresh lime juice, divided
- 4 6-oz boneless, skinless cod fillets
- 5 tbsp. dried unsweetened shredded coconut
- 8 pcs of 6-inch tortillas, heated

Directions:
1. Whisk well Chile powder, oil, and 4 tbsp. lime juice in a glass baking dish. Add cod and marinate for 12 – 15 minutes. Turning once halfway through the marinating time.
2. Make the salsa by mixing coconut, 6 tbsp. lime juice, cilantro, onions, tomatoes and mangoes in a medium bowl. Set aside.
3. On high, heat a grill pan. Place cod and grill for four minutes per side turning only once.
4. Once cooked, slice cod into large flakes and evenly divide onto tortilla.
5. Evenly divide salsa on top of cod and serve with a side of lime wedges.

Nutrition:
- Calories: 477;
- Protein: 35.0g;
- Fat: 12.4g;
- Carbs: 57.4g

95. Baked Cod Crusted with Herbs

Level of difficulty: Novice level
Preparation Time: 5 minutes
Cooking Time: 10 minutes
Servings: 4
Ingredients:
- ¼ cup honey
- ¼ teaspoon salt
- ½ cup panko
- ½ teaspoon pepper
- 1 tbsp. extra-virgin olive oil
- 1 tbsp. lemon juice
- 1 teaspoon dried basil
- 1 teaspoon dried parsley
- 1 teaspoon rosemary
- 4 pieces of 4-oz cod fillets

Directions:
1. With olive oil, grease a 9 x 13-inch baking pan and preheat oven to 375oF.
2. In a zip top bag mix panko, rosemary, salt, pepper, parsley and basil.
3. Evenly spread cod fillets in prepped dish and drizzle with lemon juice.
4. Then brush the fillets with honey on all sides. Discard remaining honey if any.
5. Then evenly divide the panko mixture on top of cod fillets.
6. Pop in the oven and bake for ten minutes or until fish is cooked. Serve and enjoy.

Nutrition:
- Calories: 137;
- Protein: 5g;
- Fat: 2g;
- Carbs: 21g

96. Cajun Garlic Shrimp Noodle Bowl

Level of difficulty: Intermediate
Preparation Time: 10 minutes
Cooking Time: 15 minutes
Servings: 2
Ingredients:
1. ½ teaspoon salt
2. 1 onion, sliced
3. 1 red pepper, sliced
4. 1 tbsp. butter
5. 1 teaspoon garlic granules
6. 1 teaspoon onion powder
7. 1 teaspoon paprika
8. 2 large zucchinis, cut into noodle strips
9. 20 jumbo shrimps, shells removed and deveined
10. 3 cloves garlic, minced
11. 3 tbsp. ghee
12. A dash of cayenne pepper
13. A dash of red pepper flakes

Directions:
1. Prepare the Cajun seasoning by mixing the onion powder, garlic granules, pepper flakes, cayenne pepper, paprika and salt. Toss in the shrimp to coat in the seasoning.
2. In a skillet, heat the ghee and sauté the garlic. Add in the red pepper and onions and continue sautéing for 4 minutes.
3. Add the Cajun shrimp and cook until opaque. Set aside.
4. In another pan, heat the butter and sauté the zucchini noodles for three minutes.
5. Assemble by the placing the Cajun shrimps on top of the zucchini noodles.

Nutrition:
- Calories: 712;
- Fat: 30.0g;
- Protein: 97.8g;
- Carbs: 20.2g

97. Crazy Saganaki Shrimp

Level of difficulty: Novice level
Preparation Time: 10 minutes
Cooking Time: 10 minutes
Servings: 4
Ingredients:
- ¼ teaspoon salt
- ½ cup Chardonnay
- ½ cup crumbled Greek feta cheese
- 1 medium bulb. fennel, cored and finely chopped
- 1 small Chile pepper, seeded and minced
- 1 tbsp. extra-virgin olive oil
- 12 jumbo shrimps, peeled and deveined with tails left on
- 2 tbsp. lemon juice, divided
- 5 scallions sliced thinly
- Pepper to taste

Directions:
1. In medium bowl, mix salt, lemon juice and shrimp.
2. On medium fire, place a saganaki pan (or large nonstick saucepan) and heat oil.
3. Sauté Chile pepper, scallions, and fennel for 4 minutes or until starting to brown and is already soft.
4. Add wine and sauté for another minute.
5. Place shrimps on top of fennel, cover and cook for 4 minutes or until shrimps are pink.
6. Remove just the shrimp and transfer to a plate.
7. Add pepper, feta and 1 tbsp. lemon juice to pan and cook for a minute or until cheese begins to melt.
8. To serve, place cheese and fennel mixture on a serving plate and top with shrimps.

Nutrition:
- Calories: 310;
- Protein: 49.7g;
- Fat: 6.8g;
- Carbs: 8.4g

98. Creamy Bacon-Fish Chowder

Level of difficulty: Novice level
Preparation Time: 10 minutes
Cooking Time: 30 minutes
Servings: 8
Ingredients:
- 1 1/2 lbs. cod
- 1 1/2 teaspoon dried thyme
- 1 large onion, chopped
- 1 medium carrot, coarsely chopped
- 1 tbsp. butter, cut into small pieces
- 1 teaspoon salt, divided
- 3 1/2 cups baking potato, peeled and cubed
- 3 slices uncooked bacon
- 3/4 teaspoon freshly ground black pepper, divided
- 4 1/2 cups water
- 4 bay leaves
- 4 cups 2% reduced-fat milk

Directions:
1. In a large skillet, add the water and bay leaves and let it simmer. Add the fish. Cover and let it simmer some more until the flesh flakes easily with fork. Remove the fish from the skillet and cut into large pieces. Set aside the cooking liquid.
2. Place Dutch oven in medium heat and cook the bacon until crisp. Remove the bacon and reserve the bacon drippings. Crush the bacon and set aside.
3. Stir potato, onion and carrot in the pan with the bacon drippings, cook over medium heat for 10 minutes. Add the

cooking liquid, bay leaves, 1/2 teaspoon salt, 1/4 teaspoon pepper and thyme, let it boil. Lower the heat and let simmer for 10 minutes. Add the milk and butter, simmer until the potatoes becomes tender, but do not boil. Add the fish, 1/2 teaspoon salt, 1/2 teaspoon pepper. Remove the bay leaves.
4. Serve sprinkled with the crushed bacon.

Nutrition:
- Calories: 400;
- Carbs: 34.5g;
- Protein: 20.8g;
- Fat: 19.7g

99. Crisped Coco-Shrimp with Mango Dip

Level of difficulty: Novice level
Preparation Time: 10 minutes
Cooking Time: 20 minutes
Servings: 4
Ingredients:
- 1 cup shredded coconut
- 1 lb. raw shrimp, peeled and deveined
- 2 egg whites
- 4 tbsp. tapioca starch
- Pepper and salt to taste
- Mango Dip Ingredients:
- 1 cup mango, chopped
- 1 jalapeño, thinly minced
- 1 teaspoon lime juice
- 1/3 cup coconut milk
- 3 teaspoon raw honey

Directions:
1. Preheat oven to 400oF.
2. Ready a pan with wire rack on top.
3. In a medium bowl, add tapioca starch and season with pepper and salt.
4. In a second medium bowl, add egg whites and whisk.
5. In a third medium bowl, add coconut.
6. To ready shrimps, dip first in tapioca starch, then egg whites, and then coconut. Place dredged shrimp on wire rack. Repeat until all shrimps are covered.
7. Pop shrimps in the oven and roast for 10 minutes per side.
8. Meanwhile make the dip by adding all ingredients in a blender. Puree until smooth and creamy. Transfer to a dipping bowl.
9. Once shrimps are golden brown, serve with mango dip.

Nutrition:
- Calories: 294.2;
- Protein: 26.6g;
- Fat: 7g;
- Carbs: 31.2g

100. Cucumber-Basil Salsa on Halibut Pouches

Level of difficulty: Novice level
Preparation Time: 10 minutes
Cooking Time: 17 minutes
Servings: 4
Ingredients:
- 1 lime, thinly sliced into 8 pieces
- 2 cups mustard greens, stems removed
- 2 teaspoon olive oil
- 4 – 5 radishes trimmed and quartered
- 4 4-oz skinless halibut filets
- 4 large fresh basil leaves
- Cayenne pepper to taste – optional
- Pepper and salt to taste

Salsa Ingredients:
- 1 ½ cups diced cucumber

- 1 ½ finely chopped fresh basil leaves
- 2 teaspoon fresh lime juice
- Pepper and salt to taste

Directions:
1. Preheat oven to 400oF.
2. Prepare parchment papers by making 4 pieces of 15 x 12-inch rectangles. Lengthwise, fold in half and unfold pieces on the table.
3. Season halibut fillets with pepper, salt and cayenne—if using cayenne.
4. Just to the right of the fold going lengthwise, place ½ cup of mustard greens. Add a basil leaf on center of mustard greens and topped with 1 lime slice. Around the greens, layer ¼ of the radishes. Drizzle with ½ teaspoon of oil, season with pepper and salt. Top it with a slice of halibut fillet.
5. Just as you would make a calzone, fold parchment paper over your filling and crimp the edges of the parchment paper beginning from one end to the other end. To seal the end of the crimped parchment paper, pinch it.
6. Repeat process to remaining ingredients until you have 4 pieces of parchment papers filled with halibut and greens.
7. Place pouches in a baking pan and bake in the oven until halibut is flaky, around 15 to 17 minutes.
8. While waiting for halibut pouches to cook, make your salsa by mixing all salsa ingredients in a medium bowl.
9. Once halibut is cooked, remove from oven and make a tear on top. Be careful of the steam as it is very hot. Equally divide salsa and spoon ¼ of salsa on top of halibut through the slit you have created.

Nutrition:
- Calories: 335.4;
- Protein: 20.2g;
- Fat: 16.3g;
- Carbs: 22.1g

101. Chicken Zucchini Boats

Level of difficulty: Intermediate
Preparation Time: 15 minutes
Cooking Time: 30 minutes
Servings: 2
Ingredients:
1. 1 zucchini
- ½ cup ground chicken
- ½ teaspoon chipotle pepper
- ½ teaspoon tomato sauce
- 1 oz. Swiss cheese, shredded
- ½ teaspoon salt
- 4 tbsp. water

Directions:
1. Trim the zucchini and cut it on 2 halves.
2. Remove the zucchini pulp.
3. In the mixing bowl mix up together ground chicken, chipotle pepper, tomato sauce, and salt.
4. Fill the zucchini with chicken mixture and top with Swiss cheese.
5. Place the zucchini boats in the tray. Add water.
6. Bake the boats for 30 minutes at 355F.

Nutrition:
- Calories 134,
- Fat 6.3 g,
- Fiber 1.1,
- Protein 13.4 g

102. Urban Chicken Alfredo

Level of difficulty: Novice level
Preparation Time: 10 minutes
Cooking Time: 20 minutes
Servings: 2
Ingredients:

- 1 onion, chopped
- 1 sweet red pepper, roasted, chopped
- 1 cup spinach, chopped
- ½ cup cream
- 1 teaspoon cream cheese
- 1 tbsp. olive oil
- ½ teaspoon ground black pepper
- 8 oz. chicken breast, skinless, boneless, sliced

Directions:
1. Mix up together sliced chicken breast with ground black pepper and put in the saucepan.
2. Add olive oil and mix up.
3. Roast the chicken for 5 minutes over the medium-high heat. Stir it from time to time.
4. After this, add chopped sweet pepper, onion, and cream cheese.
5. Mix up well and bring to boil.
6. Add spinach and cream. Mix up well.
7. Close the lid and cook chicken Alfredo for 10 minutes more over the medium heat.

Nutrition:
- Calories 279,
- Fat 14 g,
- Fiber 2.5 g,
- Protein 26.4 g

103. Grilled Chicken and Zucchini Kebabs

Level of difficulty: Novice level
Preparation Time: 10 minutes
Cooking Time: 12 minutes
Servings: 5
Ingredients:
- 2 Boneless Chicken Breasts Cut Into 1-Inch Pieces.
- 2 Medium Zucchini Sliced into Thick Rounds.
- 1 Large Red Onion Cut into 1-Inch Pieces.
- 2 Large Lemons.
- 3 Cloves Garlic Minced.
- 1 Tbsp. Chopped Fresh Thyme.
- 1 Tbsp. Chopped Fresh Rosemary.
- ¼ Cup Bertolli 100% Pure Olive Oil.
- 1 Teaspoon Kosher Salt.
- ½ Teaspoon Freshly Ground Pepper.

Directions:
1. Situate the chicken pieces in a large Ziploc bag or bowl. Put the zucchini and red onion in a separate Ziploc bag or bowl. Put aside.
2. Zest one of the lemons. Juice both lemons and mix to the lemon zest. Scourge the chopped garlic, thyme, rosemary, olive oil, salt, and pepper. Put half of the marinade into the freezer bag with the chicken pieces and fill in the other half in the freezer bag with the zucchini and onion. Marinate for 4 hours in the refrigerator.
3. Once ready, make the kebabs. Alternate chicken, zucchini, and onion on skewers. Remove any remaining marinade.
4. Slightly grease the grill with olive oil then preheat to medium heat.
5. Grill chicken kebabs, flipping often so each side browns and has light grill marks, about 10-12 minutes or until chicken is cooked through. Serve immediately.

Nutrition:
- Calories: 78
- Protein: 1.62g
- Fat: 5.54g

104. Gyro Burgers with Tahini Sauce

Level of difficulty: Novice level
Preparation Time: 10 minutes
Cooking Time: 12 minutes
Servings: 4
Ingredients:
- 1-Pound Extra-Lean Ground Beef.
- 1 Teaspoon Greek Seasoning.
- 4 Pita Rounds.
- 4 Lettuce Leaves.
- 8 Large Tomato Slices.
- 4 Thin Red Onion Slices.
- Tahini Sauce.
- 1/4 Cup Feta Cheese.

Directions:
1. Combine beef and seasoning. Shape into 4 patties.
2. Grill, close, over medium-high heat (350° to 400°) 7 minutes on each side.
3. Slice off 2 inches of bread from 1 side of each pita round, forming a pocket. Lay each with 1 lettuce leaf, 2 tomato slices, and 1 red onion slice. Mix in burger. Pour in 2 tbsp. Tahini Sauce, and garnish with 1 tbsp. cheese.

Nutrition:
- Calories: 297
- Protein: 29.42g
- Fat: 17.83g

105. Baked Parmesan Chicken Wraps

Level of difficulty: Novice level
Preparation Time: 10 minutes
Cooking Time: 3 minutes
Servings: 4.
Ingredients:
- 3 Cups Skinless Chicken Breasts
- 1 1/2 Teaspoons Italian Seasoning
- 1/2 Teaspoon Kosher Salt.
- 1/8 Teaspoon Black Pepper.
- 1 Cup Your Favorite Marinara Sauce.
- 1/4 Cup Finely Chopped Fresh Basil.
- 4 Flat-out Flatbreads
- 1 Cup Reduced-Fat Italian Cheese Blend.
- Extra Marinara Sauce, Warmed for Dipping

Directions:
1. Situate shredded chicken in a medium bowl. Mix Italian seasoning, salt, and black pepper.
2. Pour in marinara sauce and basil to the chicken mixture, and stir to combine again.
3. Lay 1 flatbread on a work surface, and drizzle 1/4 cup of cheese down the center, leaving a large border all around the cheese. Arrange 1/4 of the chicken mixture on top of the cheese.
4. Crease short ends of the flatbread inward toward the middle, and then fold the long sides of the flatbread inward toward the middle, making a secured wrap.
5. Do it with the remaining 3 flatbreads, dividing the remaining cheese and the remaining chicken mixture evenly among them.
6. Prep a dry nonstick skillet over medium heat. Once preheated, add the wraps and cook on the first side until golden brown, about 1 1/2 - 2 minutes. Turn the wraps and cook on the second side until golden, about another 1 1/2 minutes.
7. Drizzle with marinara sauce for dipping.

Nutrition:
- Calories: 102
- Protein: 8.02g
- Fat: 5.56g

106. Greek Flavor Tomato Chicken Pasta

Level of difficulty: Novice level
Preparation Time: 20 minutes
Cooking Time: 3 hours 20minutes
Servings: 4
Ingredients:
- 3 Tbsp. Olive Oil.
- 1 Pound (454 G) Boneless, Skinless Chicken Breasts, Cut Into 1-Inch Cubes.
- 15 Ounces (425 G) Tomatoes, Diced.
- 2 Medium Carrots
- 1½ Cups Freshly Squeezed Tomato Juice.
- 1½ Cups Low-Sodium Chicken Broth.
- 1 Stalk Celery
- 1 Medium Onion, Cut into Wedges.
- ½ Teaspoon Rosemary.
- ½ Teaspoon Thyme.
- 1 Teaspoon Basil.
- 1 Teaspoon Oregano.
- ½ Teaspoon Ground Cinnamon.
- ½ Teaspoon Sea Salt.
- 1 Cup Uncooked Medium Shell Pasta.
- 1 Cup Feta Cheese Crumbled.

Directions:
1. Brush the insert of the slow cooker with 2 tbsp. of olive oil.
2. Heat the remaining olive oil in a nonstick skillet at medium-high heat.
3. Stir in the chicken to the skillet and cook for 6 minutes. Shake the skillet periodically during the cooking.
4. Situate the chicken to a plate, and pat dry with paper towels, then move them into the slow cooker.
5. Add the tomatoes, carrots, tomato juice, chicken stock, celery, and onion to the slow cooker. Season with rosemary, thyme, basil, oregano, cinnamon, and salt. Stir to mix well.
6. Situate the slow cooker lid on and cook on HIGH for 2 hours and 30 minutes.
7. Add the pasta to the slow cooker. Put the lid on and cook for an additional 40 minutes or until the pasta is al dente.
8. Serve the pasta, chicken, and vegetables on a large plate, and spread the feta cheese on top before serving.

Nutrition:
- Calories 581
- Fat: 32.4g
- Protein: 29.4g

107. Spinach and Feta-Stuffed Chicken Breasts

Level of difficulty: Intermediate
Preparation Time: 10 minutes
Cooking Time: 45 minutes
Servings: 4
Ingredients:
- 2 tbsp. extra-virgin olive oil
- 1-pound fresh baby spinach
- 3 garlic cloves, minced
- Zest of 1 lemon
- ½ teaspoon sea salt
- 1/8 teaspoon freshly ground black pepper
- ½ cup crumbled feta cheese
- 4 boneless, chicken breast halves

Directions:
1. Preheat the oven to 350°F.
2. Using big skillet over medium-high heat, heat the olive oil until it shimmers.
3. Add the spinach. Cook for 6 minutes.
4. Mix in the garlic, lemon zest, sea salt, and pepper. Cook for 30 seconds, stirring constantly. Cool slightly and mix in the cheese.

5. Spread the spinach and cheese mixture in an even layer over the chicken pieces and roll the breast around the filling. Hold closed with toothpicks or butcher's twine.
6. Place the breasts in a 9-by-13-inch baking dish and bake for 30 to 40 minutes. Remove from the oven and let rest for 5 minutes before slicing and serving.

Nutrition:
- Calories: 263
- Protein: 17g
- Fat: 20g

108. Mango Chicken Salad

Level of difficulty: Novice level
Preparation Time: 10 minutes
Cooking Time: 12 minutes
Servings: 3
Ingredients:
- 1 cup lettuce, chopped
- 1 cup arugula, chopped
- 1 mango, peeled, chopped
- 8 oz. chicken breast, skinless, boneless
- 1 tbsp. lime juice
- 1 teaspoon sesame oil
- ½ teaspoon salt
- ½ teaspoon ground black pepper
- 1 teaspoon butter

Directions:
1. Sprinkle the chicken breast with salt and ground black pepper.
2. Melt butter in the skillet and add chicken breast.
3. Roast it for 10 minutes over the medium heat. Flip it on another side from time to time.
4. Meanwhile, combine together lettuce, arugula, mango, and sesame oil in the salad bowl.
5. Add lime juice.
6. Chop the cooked chicken breast roughly and chill it to the room temperature.
7. Add it in the mango salad and mix up.

Nutrition:
- Calories 183,
- Fat 5.2 g,
- Fiber 2.8 g,
- Carbs 17.4 g,
- Protein 17.2 g

109. Tender Chicken Quesadilla

Level of difficulty: Novice level
Preparation Time: 10 minutes
Cooking Time: 20 minutes
Servings: 4
Ingredients:
- 2 bread tortillas
- 1 teaspoon butter
- 2 teaspoons olive oil
- 1 teaspoon Taco seasoning
- 6 oz. chicken breast, skinless, boneless, sliced
- 1/3 cup Cheddar cheese, shredded
- 1 bell pepper, cut on the wedges

Directions:
1. Pour 1 teaspoon of olive oil in the skillet and add chicken.
2. Sprinkle the meat with Taco seasoning and mix up well.
3. Roast chicken for 10 minutes over the medium heat. Stir it from time to time.
4. Then transfer the cooked chicken in the plate.
5. Add remaining olive oil in the skillet.
6. Then add bell pepper and roast it for 5 minutes. Stir it all the time.
7. Mix up together bell pepper with chicken.
8. Toss butter in the skillet and melt it.

9. Put 1 tortilla in the skillet.
10. Put Cheddar cheese on the tortilla and flatten it.
11. Then add chicken-pepper mixture and cover it with the second tortilla.
12. Roast the quesadilla for 2 minutes from each side.
13. Cut the cooked meal on the halves and transfer in the serving plates.

Nutrition:
- Calories 167,
- Fat 8.2 g,
- Fiber 0.8 g,
- Carbs 16.4 g,
- Protein 24.2 g

110. Chicken Bolognese

Level of difficulty: Novice level
Preparation Time: 7 minutes
Cooking Time: 25 minutes
Servings: 4
Ingredients:
- 1 cup ground chicken
- 2 oz. Parmesan, grated
- 1 tbsp. olive oil
- 2 tbsp. fresh parsley, chopped
- 1 teaspoon chili pepper
- 1 teaspoon paprika
- ½ teaspoon dried oregano
- ¼ teaspoon garlic, minced
- ½ teaspoon dried thyme
- 1/3 cup crushed tomatoes

Directions:
1. Heat up olive oil in the skillet.
2. Add ground chicken and sprinkle it with chili pepper, paprika, dried oregano, dried thyme, and parsley. Mix up well.
3. Cook the chicken for 5 minutes and add crushed tomatoes. Mix up well.
4. Close the lid and simmer the chicken mixture for 10 minutes over the low heat.
5. Then add grated Parmesan and mix up.
6. Cook chicken bolognese for 5 minutes more over the medium heat.

Nutrition:
- Calories 154,
- Fat 9.3 g,
- Fiber 1.1,
- Carbs 3 g,
- Protein 15.4 g

111. Jerk Chicken

Level of difficulty: Novice level
Preparation Time: 10 minutes
Cooking Time: 30 minutes
Servings: 2
Ingredients:
- 2 chicken thighs, skinless, boneless
- 1 teaspoon fresh ginger, chopped
- 1 garlic clove, chopped
- ½ spring onion, chopped
- 1 teaspoon liquid honey
- 1 teaspoon fresh parsley, chopped
- 1 teaspoon fresh coriander, chopped
- ¼ teaspoon chili flakes
- ¼ teaspoon ground black pepper
- 2 teaspoons lemon juice

Directions:
1. Mix up together fresh ginger, garlic, onion, liquid honey, parsley, coriander, chili flakes, and ground black pepper.
2. Rub the chicken thighs with honey mixture generously.
3. Preheat the grill to 385F.
4. Place the chicken thighs in the grill and cook for 30 minutes. Flip the chicken thighs on another side after 15 minutes of cooking. The cooked jerk chicken should have a brown crust.

5. Sprinkle the cooked chicken with lemon juice.

Nutrition:
- Calories 139,
- Fat 7.3 g,
- Fiber 0.1,
- Carbs 4 g,
- Protein 19.4 g

112. Pomegranate Chicken Thighs

Level of difficulty: Novice level
Preparation Time: 10 minutes
Cooking Time: 10 minutes
Servings: 2
Ingredients:
- 1 tbsp. pomegranate molasses
- 8 oz. chicken thighs (4 oz. each chicken thigh)
- ½ teaspoon paprika
- 1 teaspoon cornstarch
- ½ teaspoon chili flakes
- ½ teaspoon ground black pepper
- 1 teaspoon olive oil
- ½ teaspoon lime juice

Directions:
1. In the shallow bowl mix up together ground black pepper, chili flakes, paprika, and cornstarch.
2. Rub the chicken thighs with spice mixture.
3. Heat up olive oil in the skillet.
4. Add chicken thighs and roast them for 4 minutes from each side over the medium heat.
5. When the chicken thighs are light brown, sprinkle them with pomegranate molasses and roast for 1 minute from each side.

Nutrition:
- Calories 374,
- Fat 21.3 g,
- Fiber 0.1,
- Carbs 9 g,
- Protein 30.4 g

113. Butter Chicken

Level of difficulty: Novice level
Preparation Time: 15 minutes
Cooking Time: 30 minutes
Servings: 5
Ingredients:
- 1-pound chicken fillet
- 1/3 cup butter, softened
- 1 tbsp. rosemary
- ½ teaspoon thyme
- 1 teaspoon salt
- ½ lemon

Directions:
1. Churn together thyme, salt, and rosemary.
2. Chop the chicken fillet roughly and mix up with churned butter mixture.
3. Place the prepared chicken in the baking dish.
4. Squeeze the lemon over the chicken.
5. Chop the squeezed lemon and add in the baking dish.
6. Cover the chicken with foil and bake it for 20 minutes at 365F.
7. Then discard the foil and bake the chicken for 10 minutes more.

Nutrition:
- Calories 254,
- Fat 19.3 g,
- Fiber 1.1,
- Carbs 1 g,
- Protein 36.4 g

114. Mediterranean Pearl Couscous

Level of difficulty: Novice level
Preparation Time: 4 minutes
Cooking Time: 10 minutes
Servings: 6
Ingredients:
For the Lemon Dill Vinaigrette:
- 1 large lemon, juice of
- 1/3 cup Extra virgin olive oil
- 1 tsp dill weed
- 1 tsp garlic powder
- Salt and pepper

For the Israeli Couscous:
- 2 cups Pearl Couscous, Israeli Couscous
- Extra virgin olive oil
- 2 cups grape tomatoes, halved
- 1/3 cup finely chopped red onions
- 1/2 English cucumber
- 15 oz. can chickpeas
- 14 oz. can good quality artichoke hearts
- 1/2 cup Kalamata olives
- 15–20 fresh basil leaves
- 3 oz. fresh baby mozzarella or feta cheese

Directions:
1. Make the lemon-dill vinaigrette, scourge lemon juice, olive oil, dill weed, garlic powder, salt and pepper then keep aside
2. In a medium-sized heavy pot, heat two tbsp. of olive oil
3. Sauté the couscous in the olive oil briefly until golden brown, then add cups of boiling water (or follow the instructed on the package), and cook according to package.
4. Once done, drain in a colander, set aside in a bowl and allow to cool
5. In a large mixing bowl, combine the extra virgin olive oil, grape tomatoes, red onions, cucumber, chickpeas, artichoke hearts, and Kalamata olives
6. Then add in the couscous and the basil, mix together gently
7. Now, give the lemon-dill vinaigrette a quick whisk and add to the couscous salad, mix to combine
8. Taste and adjust salt, if needed
9. Distribute among the containers, store for 2-3 days
10. To Serve: Add in the mozzarella cheese, garnish with more fresh basil and enjoy!

Nutrition:
- Calories: 393
- Fat: 13g
- Protein: 13g

115. Potato and Tuna Salad

Level of difficulty: Novice level
Preparation Time: 18 minutes
Cooking Time: 0 minutes
Servings: 4
Ingredients:
- 1-pound baby potatoes, scrubbed, boiled
- 1 cup tuna chunks, drained
- 1 cup cherry tomatoes, halved
- 1 cup medium onion, thinly sliced
- 8 pitted black olives
- 2 medium hard-boiled eggs, sliced
- 1 head Romaine lettuce
- Honey lemon mustard dressing
- 1/4 cup olive oil
- 2 tbsp. lemon juice
- 1 tbsp. Dijon mustard
- 1 teaspoon dill weed, chopped
- Salt as needed
- Pepper as needed

Directions:
1. Take a small glass bowl and mix in your olive oil, honey, lemon juice, Dijon mustard and dill
2. Season the mix with pepper and salt
3. Add in the tuna, baby potatoes, cherry tomatoes, red onion, green beans, black olives and toss everything nicely
4. Arrange your lettuce leaves on a beautiful serving dish to make the base of your salad
5. Top them up with your salad mixture and place the egg slices
6. Drizzle it with the previously prepared Salad Dressing
7. Serve

Nutrition:
- Calories: 406
- Fat: 22g
- Protein: 26g

116. Tuna with Vegetable Mix

Level of difficulty: Novice level
Preparation Time: 8 minutes
Cooking Time: 16 minutes
Servings: 4
Ingredients:
- ¼ cup extra-virgin olive oil, divided
- 1 tbsp. rice vinegar
- 1 teaspoon kosher salt, divided
- ¾ teaspoon Dijon mustard
- ¾ teaspoon honey
- 4 ounces baby gold beets, thinly sliced
- 4 ounces fennel bulb, trimmed and thinly sliced
- 4 ounces baby turnips, thinly sliced
- 6 ounces Granny Smith apple, very thinly sliced
- 2 teaspoons sesame seeds, toasted
- 6 ounces tuna steaks
- ½ teaspoon black pepper
- 1 tbsp. fennel fronds, torn

Directions:
1. Scourge 2 tbsp. of oil, ½ a teaspoon of salt, honey, vinegar, and mustard.
2. Give the mixture a nice mix.
3. Add fennel, beets, apple, and turnips; mix and toss until everything is evenly coated.
4. Sprinkle with sesame seeds and toss well.
5. Using cast-iron skillet, heat 2 tbsp. of oil over high heat.
6. Carefully season the tuna with ½ a teaspoon of salt and pepper
7. Situate the tuna in the skillet and cook for 4 minutes, giving 1½ minutes per side.
8. Remove the tuna and slice it up.
9. Place in containers with the vegetable mix.
10. Serve with the fennel mix, and enjoy!

Nutrition:
- Calories: 443
- Fat: 17.1g
- Protein: 16.5g

117. Tuna Bowl with Kale

Level of difficulty: Novice level
Preparation Time: 4 minutes
Cooking Time: 18 minutes
Servings: 6
Ingredients:
- 3 tbsp. extra virgin olive oil
- 1 ½ teaspoons minced garlic
- ¼ cup of capers
- 2 teaspoons sugar
- 15 ounce can of drained and rinsed great northern beans
- 1-pound chopped kale with the center ribs removed
- ½ teaspoon ground black pepper

- 1 cup chopped onion
- 2 ½ ounces of drained sliced olives
- ¼ teaspoon sea salt
- ¼ teaspoon crushed red pepper
- 6 ounces of tuna in olive oil, do not drain

Directions:
1. Place a large pot, like a stockpot, on your stove and turn the burner to high heat.
2. Fill the pot about 3-quarters of the way full with water and let it come to a boil.
3. Cook the kale for 2 minutes.
4. Drain the kale and set it aside.
5. Set the heat to medium and place the empty pot back on the burner.
6. Add the oil and onion. Sauté for 3 to 4 minutes.
7. Combine the garlic into the oil mixture and sauté for another minute.
8. Add the capers, olives, and red pepper.
9. Cook the ingredients for another minute while stirring.
10. Pour in the sugar and stir while you toss in the kale. Mix all the ingredients thoroughly and ensure the kale is thoroughly coated.
11. Cover the pot and set the timer for 8 minutes.
12. Put off the heat and stir in the tuna, pepper, beans, salt, and any other herbs that will make this one of the best Mediterranean dishes you've ever made.

Nutrition:
- Calories: 265
- Fats: 12g
- Protein: 16g

118. Greek Baked Cod

Level of difficulty: Intermediate

Preparation Time: 9 minutes
Cooking Time: 13 minutes
Servings: 4
Ingredients:
- 1 ½ lb. Cod fillet pieces (4–6 pieces)
- 5 garlic cloves, peeled and minced
- 1/4 cup chopped fresh parsley leaves
- Lemon Juice Mixture:
- 5 tbsp. fresh lemon juice
- 5 tbsp. extra virgin olive oil
- 2 tbsp. melted vegan butter

For Coating:
- 1/3 cup all-purpose flour
- 1 tsp ground coriander
- 3/4 tsp sweet Spanish paprika
- 3/4 tsp ground cumin
- 3/4 tsp salt
- 1/2 tsp black pepper

Directions:
1. Preheat oven to 400F
2. Scourge lemon juice, olive oil, and melted butter, set aside
3. In another shallow bowl, mix all-purpose flour, spices, salt and pepper, set next to the lemon bowl to create a station
4. Pat the fish fillet dry, then dip the fish in the lemon juice mixture then dip it in the flour mixture, brush off extra flour
5. In a cast iron skillet over medium-high heat, add 2 tbsp. olive oil
6. Once heated, add in the fish and sear on each side for color, but do not thoroughly cook, remove from heat
7. With the remaining lemon juice mixture, add the minced garlic and mix
8. Drizzle all over the fish fillets
9. Bake for 10 minutes, for until the it begins to flake easily with a fork
10. Allow the dish to cool completely

11. Distribute among the containers, store for 2-3 days
12. To Serve: Reheat in the microwave for 1-2 minutes or until heated through. Sprinkle chopped parsley. Enjoy!

Nutrition:
- Calories: 321
- Fat: 18g
- Protein: 23g

119. Poultry and Meat 2 Tender Lamb Chops

Level of difficulty: Novice level
Preparation Time: 10 minutes
Cooking Time: 6 hours
Servings: 8
Ingredients:
- 8 lamb chops
- ½ teaspoon dried thyme
- 1 onion, sliced
- 1 teaspoon dried oregano
- 2 garlic cloves, minced
- Pepper and salt

Directions:
1. Add sliced onion into the slow cooker.
2. Combine together thyme, oregano, pepper, and salt. Rub over lamb chops.
3. Place lamb chops in slow cooker and top with garlic.
4. Pour ¼ cup water around the lamb chops.
5. Cover and cook on low for 6 hours.
6. Serve and enjoy.

Nutrition:
- Calories 40
- Fat 1.9 g
- Carbohydrates 2.3 g
- Sugar 0.6 g
- Protein 3.4 g
- Cholesterol 0 mg

120. Seasoned Pork Chops

Level of difficulty: Novice level
Preparation Time: 10 minutes
Cooking Time: 4 hours
Servings: 4
Ingredients:
- 4 pork chops
- 2 garlic cloves, minced
- 1 cup chicken broth
- 1 tbsp. poultry seasoning
- 1/4 cup olive oil
- Pepper and salt

Directions:
1. In a bowl, whisk together olive oil, poultry seasoning, garlic, broth, pepper, and salt.
2. Pour olive oil mixture into the slow cooker then place pork chops to the crock pot.
3. Cover and cook on high for 4 hours.
4. Serve and enjoy.

Nutrition:
- Calories 386
- Fat 32.9 g
- Carbohydrates 3 g
- Sugar 1 g
- Protein 20 g
- Cholesterol 70 mg

CHAPTER 5. SNACKS

121. Chocolate Matcha Balls

Level of difficulty: Novice level
Preparation Time: 10 minutes
Cooking Time: 5 minutes
Servings: 15
Ingredients:
- 2 tbsp. unsweetened cocoa powder
- 3 tbsp. oats, gluten-free
- ½ cup pine nuts
- ½ cup almonds
- 1 cup dates, pitted
- 2 tbsp. matcha powder

Directions:
1. Add oats, pine nuts, almonds, and dates into a food processor and process until well combined.
2. Place matcha powder in a small dish.
3. Make small balls from mixture and coat with matcha powder.
4. Enjoy or store in refrigerator until ready to eat.

Nutrition:
- Calories 88,
- Fat 4.9g,
- Carbs 11.3g,
- Protein 1.9g

122. Chia Almond Butter Pudding

Level of difficulty: Intermediate
Preparation Time: 5 minutes
Cooking Time: 5 minutes
Servings: 1
Ingredients:
- ¼ cup chia seeds
- 1 cup unsweetened almond milk
- 1 ½ tbsp. maple syrup
- 2 ½ tbsp. almond butter

Directions:
1. Add almond milk, maple syrup, and almond butter in a bowl and stir well.
2. Add chia seeds and stir to mix.
3. Pour pudding mixture into the Mason jar and place in the refrigerator for overnight.
4. Serve and enjoy.

Nutrition:
- Calories 354,
- Fat 21.3g,
- Carbs 31.1g,
- Protein 11.2g,

123. Refreshing Strawberry Popsicles

Level of difficulty: Novice level
Preparation Time: 5 minutes
Cooking Time: 5 minutes
Servings: 8
Ingredients:
- ½ cup almond milk
- 2 ½ cup fresh strawberries

Directions:
1. Add strawberries and almond milk into the blender and blend until smooth.
2. Pour strawberry mixture into popsicles molds and place in the refrigerator for 4 hours or until set.
3. Serve and enjoy.

Nutrition:
- Calories 49,
- Fat 3.7g,
- Carbs 4.3g,
- Protein 0.6g,

124. Dark Chocolate Mousse

Level of difficulty: Novice level
Preparation Time: 10 minutes
Cooking Time: 10 minutes
Servings: 4
Ingredients:
- 3.5oz unsweetened dark chocolate, grated
- ½ tsp. vanilla
- 1 tbsp. honey
- 2 cups Greek yogurt
- ¾ cup unsweetened almond milk

Directions:
1. Add chocolate and almond milk in a saucepan and heat over medium heat until just chocolate melted. Do not boil.
2. Once the chocolate and almond milk combined then add vanilla and honey and stir well.
3. Add yogurt in a large mixing bowl.
4. Pour chocolate mixture on top of yogurt and mix until well combined.
5. Pour chocolate yogurt mixture into the serving bowls and place in refrigerator for 2 hours.
6. Top with fresh raspberries and serve.

Nutrition:
- Calories 278,
- Fat 15.4g,
- Carbs 20g,
- Protein 10.5g,

125. Warm & Soft Baked Pears

Level of difficulty: Novice level
Preparation Time: 10 minutes
Cooking Time: 25 minutes
Servings: 4
Ingredients:
- 4 pears, cut in half and core
- ½ tsp. vanilla
- ¼ tsp. cinnamon
- ½ cup maple syrup

Directions:
1. Preheat the oven to 375°F.
2. Spray a baking tray with cooking spray.
3. Arrange pears, cut side up on a prepared baking tray and sprinkle with cinnamon.
4. In a small bowl, whisk vanilla and maple syrup and drizzle over pears.
5. Bake pears in preheated oven for 25 minutes.
6. Serve and enjoy.

Nutrition:
- Calories 226,
- Fat 0.4g,
- Carbs 58.4g,
- Sugar 43.9g,
- Protein 0.8g,

126. Healthy & Quick Energy Bites

Level of difficulty: Novice level
Preparation Time: 10 minutes
Cooking Time: 0 minutes
Servings: 20
Ingredients:
- 2 cups cashew nuts
- ¼ tsp. cinnamon
- 1 tsp. lemon zest
- 4 tbsp. dates, chopped
- 1/3 cup unsweetened shredded coconut
- ¾ cup dried apricots

Directions:
1. Line baking tray with parchment paper and set aside.
2. Add all ingredients in a food processor and process until the mixture is crumbly and well combined.

3. Make small balls from mixture and place on a prepared baking tray.
4. Place in refrigerator for 1 hour.
5. Serve and enjoy.

Nutrition:
- Calories 100,
- Fat 7.5g,
- Carbs 7.2g,
- Protein 2.4g,

127. Creamy Yogurt Banana Bowls

Level of difficulty: Novice level
Preparation Time: 10 minutes
Cooking Time: 0 minutes
Servings: 4
Ingredients:
- 2 bananas, sliced
- ½ tsp. ground nutmeg
- 3 tbsp. flaxseed meal
- ¼ cup creamy peanut butter
- 4 cups Greek yogurt

Directions:
1. Divide Greek yogurt between 4 serving bowls and top with sliced bananas.
2. Add peanut butter in microwave-safe bowl and microwave for 30 seconds.
3. Drizzle 1 tbsp. of melted peanut butter on each bowl on top of the sliced bananas.
4. Sprinkle cinnamon and flax meal on top and serve.

Nutrition:
- Calories 351,
- Fat 13.1g,
- Carbs 35.6g,
- Protein 19.6g,

128. Chicken Wings Platter

Level of difficulty: Intermediate
Preparation Time: 10 minutes
Cooking Time: 20 minutes
Servings: 4
Ingredients:
- 2 lb. chicken wings
- ½ cup tomato sauce
- A pinch of salt and black pepper
- 1 tsp. smoked paprika
- 1 tbsp. cilantro, chopped
- 1 tbsp. chives, chopped

Directions:
1. In your instant pot, combine the chicken wings with the sauce and the rest of the ingredients, stir, put the lid on and cook on High for 20 minutes.
2. Release the pressure naturally for 10 minutes, arrange the chicken wings on a platter and serve as an appetizer.

Nutrition:
- Calories 203,
- Fat 13g,
- Fiber 3g,
- Carbs 5g,
- Protein 8g

129. Carrot Spread

Level of difficulty: Novice level
Preparation Time: 10 minutes
Cooking Time: 10 minutes
Servings: 4
Ingredients:
- ¼ cup veggie stock
- A pinch of salt and black pepper
- 1 tsp. onion powder
- ½ tsp. garlic powder
- ½ tsp. oregano, dried
- 1 lb. carrots, sliced
- ½ cup coconut cream

Directions:
1. In your instant pot, combine all the ingredients except the cream, put the

lid on and cook on High for 10 minutes.
2. Release the pressure naturally for 10 minutes, transfer the carrots mix to food processor, add the cream, pulse well, divide into bowls and serve cold.

Nutrition:
- Calories 124,
- Fat 1g,
- Fiber 2g,
- Carbs 5g,
- Protein 8g

130. Chocolate Mousse

Level of difficulty: Novice level
Preparation Time: 10 minutes
Cooking Time: 6 minutes
Servings: 5

Ingredients:
- 4 egg yolks
- ½ tsp. vanilla
- ½ cup unsweetened almond milk
- 1 cup whipping cream
- ¼ cup cocoa powder
- ¼ cup water
- ½ cup Swerve
- 1/8 tsp. salt

Directions:
1. Add egg yolks to a large bowl and whisk until well beaten.
2. In a saucepan, add swerve, cocoa powder, and water and whisk until well combined.
3. Add almond milk and cream to the saucepan and whisk until well mix.
4. Once saucepan mixtures are heated up then turn off the heat.
5. Add vanilla and salt and stir well.
6. Add a tbsp. of chocolate mixture into the eggs and whisk until well combined.
7. Slowly pour remaining chocolate to the eggs and whisk until well combined.
8. Pour batter into the ramekins.
9. Pour 1 ½ cups of water into the instant pot then place a trivet in the pot.
10. Place ramekins on a trivet.
11. Seal pot with lid and select manual and set timer for 6 minutes.
12. Release pressure using quick release method than open the lid.
13. Carefully remove ramekins from the instant pot and let them cool completely.
14. Serve and enjoy.

Nutrition:
- Calories 128,
- Fat 11.9g,
- Carbs 4g,
- Protein 3.6g

131. Veggie Fritters

Level of difficulty: Novice level
Preparation Time: 10 minutes
Cooking Time: 10 minutes
Servings: 4

Ingredients:
- 2 garlic cloves, minced
- 2 yellow onions, chopped
- 4 scallions, chopped
- 2 carrots, grated
- 2 tsp. cumin, ground
- ½ tsp. turmeric powder
- Salt and black pepper to the taste
- ¼ tsp. coriander, ground
- 2 tbsp. parsley, chopped
- ¼ tsp. lemon juice
- ½ cup almond flour
- 2 beets, peeled and grated
- 2 eggs, whisked
- ¼ cup tapioca flour
- 3 tbsp. olive oil

Directions:
1. In a bowl, combine the garlic with the onions, scallions and the rest of the ingredients except the oil, stir well and shape medium fritters out of this mix.
2. Heat up a pan with the oil over medium-high heat, add the fritters, cook for 5 minutes on each side, arrange on a platter and serve.

Nutrition:
- Calories 209;
- Fat 11.2 g;
- Fiber 3 g;
- Carbs 4.4 g;
- Protein 4.8 g

132. White Bean Dip

Level of difficulty: Novice level
Preparation Time: 10 minutes
Cooking Time: 0 minute
Servings: 4
Ingredients:
- 15 oz. canned white beans, drained and rinsed
- 6 oz. canned artichoke hearts, drained and quartered
- 4 garlic cloves, minced
- 1 tbsp. basil, chopped
- 2 tbsp. olive oil
- Juice of ½ lemon
- Zest of ½ lemon, grated
- Salt and black pepper to the taste

Directions:
1. In your food processor, combine the beans with the artichokes and the rest of the ingredients except the oil and pulse well.
2. Add the oil gradually, pulse the mix again, divide into cups and serve as a party dip.

Nutrition:
- Calories 274;
- Fat 11.7 g;
- Carbs 18.5 g;
- Protein 16.5 g

133. Eggplant Dip

Level of difficulty: Intermediate
Preparation Time: 10 minutes
Cooking Time: 40 minutes
Servings: 4
Ingredients:
- 1 eggplant, poked with a fork
- 2 tbsp. tahini paste
- 2 tbsp. lemon juice
- 2 garlic cloves, minced
- 1 tbsp. olive oil
- Salt and black pepper to the taste
- 1 tbsp. parsley, chopped

Directions:
1. Put the eggplant in a roasting pan, bake at 400° F for 40 minutes, cool down, peel and transfer to your food processor.
2. Add the rest of the ingredients except the parsley, pulse well, divide into small bowls and serve as an appetizer with the parsley sprinkled on top.

Nutrition:
- Calories 121;
- Fat 4.3 g;
- Carbs 1.4 g;
- Protein 4.3 g

134. Bulgur Lamb Meatballs

Level of difficulty: Novice level
Preparation Time: 10 minutes
Cooking Time: 15 minutes
Servings: 6
Ingredients:
- 1 and ½ cups Greek yogurt
- ½ tsp. cumin, ground

- 1 cup cucumber, shredded
- ½ tsp. garlic, minced
- A pinch of salt and black pepper
- 1 cup bulgur
- 2 cups water
- 1 lb. lamb, ground
- ¼ cup parsley, chopped
- ¼ cup shallots, chopped
- ½ tsp. allspice, ground
- ½ tsp. cinnamon powder
- 1 tbsp. olive oil

Directions:
1. In a bowl, combine the bulgur with the water, cover the bowl, leave aside for 10 minutes, drain and transfer to a bowl.
2. Add the meat, the yogurt and the rest of the ingredients except the oil, stir well and shape medium meatballs out of this mix.
3. Heat up a pan with the oil over medium-high heat, add the meatballs, cook them for 7 minutes on each side, arrange them all on a platter and serve as an appetizer.

Nutrition:
- Calories 300;
- Fat 9.6 g;
- Carbs 22.6 g;
- Protein 6.6 g

135. Roasted Parmesan Broccoli

Level of difficulty: Novice level
Preparation Time: 10 Minutes
Cooking Time: 10 Minutes
Servings: 4
Ingredients:
- Two heads broccoli, cut into small florets
- Two tbsp. extra-virgin olive oil
- Two teaspoons minced garlic
- Zest of 1 lemon
- Juice of 1 lemon
- Pinch sea salt
- ½ cup grated Parmesan cheese

Directions:
1. Preheat the oven to 400°F.
2. Lightly grease a baking sheet using olive oil and set aside.
3. In a large bowl, toss the broccoli with the two tbsp. of olive oil, garlic, lemon zest, lemon juice, and sea salt
4. Spread the combination on the baking sheet in a single layer and sprinkle with the Parmesan cheese.
5. Bake for about 10 minutes, or until tender. Transfer the broccoli to a serving dish and serve.

Nutrition:
- Calories: 154;
- Total Fat: 11g;
- Saturated Fat: 3g;
- Carbohydrates: 10g;
- Fiber: 4;
- Protein: 9g

136. Cucumber Hummus Sandwiches

Level of difficulty: Novice level
Preparation Time: 5 Minutes
Cooking Time: 0 Minutes
Servings: 1
Ingredients:
- 10 round slices of cucumber
- Five teaspoons hummus

Directions:
1. Add one teaspoon hummus to one slice of cucumber.
2. Top with another slice and serve.

Nutrition:
- Calories 54

- Fat 21g
- Total Carbs 7g
- Protein 2g

137. Banana Strawberry Popsicles

Level of difficulty: Novice level
Preparation Time: 5 minutes
Cooking Time: 0 minutes
Servings: 8
Ingredients:
- ½ cup Greek yogurt
- 1 banana, peeled and sliced
- 1 ¼ cup fresh strawberries
- ¼ cup of water

Directions:
1. Add all ingredients into the blender and blend until smooth.
2. Pour blended mixture into the popsicles molds and place in the refrigerator for 4 hours or until set.
3. Serve and enjoy.

Nutrition:
- Calories 31,
- Fat 0. G,
- Carbohydrates 6.2g,
- Sugar 4g,
- Protein 1.2g,
- Cholesterol 1mg

138. Cajun Walnuts and Olives Bowls

Level of difficulty: Intermediate
Preparation Time: 10 minutes
Cooking Time: 10 minutes
Servings: 2
Ingredients:
- ½ pound walnuts, chopped
- A pinch of salt and black pepper
- 1 and ½ cups black olives, pitted
- ½ tbsp. Cajun seasoning
- 2 garlic cloves, minced
- 1 red chili pepper, chopped
- ¼ cup veggie stock
- 2 tbsp. tomato puree

Directions:
1. In your instant pot, combine the walnuts with the olives and the rest of the ingredients, put the lid on and cook on High 10 minutes.
2. Release the pressure fast for 5 minutes, divide the mix into small bowls and serve as an appetizer.

Nutrition:
- Calories 105,
- Fat 1g,
- Fiber 1g,
- Carbs 4g,
- Protein 7g

139. Mango Salsa

Level of difficulty: Novice level
Preparation Time: 10 minutes
Cooking Time: 10 minutes
Servings: 2
Ingredients:
- 2 mangoes, peeled and cubed
- ½ tbsp. sweet paprika
- 2 garlic cloves, minced
- 2 tbsp. cilantro, chopped
- 1 tbsp. spring onions, chopped
- 1 cup cherry tomatoes, cubed
- 1 cup avocado, peeled, pitted and cubed
- A pinch of salt and black pepper
- 1 tbsp. olive oil
- ¼ cup tomato puree
- ½ cup kalamata olives, pitted and sliced

Directions:

1. In your instant pot, combine the mangoes with the paprika and the rest of the ingredients except the cilantro, put the lid on and cook on High for 5 minutes.
2. Release the pressure fast for 5 minutes, divide the mix into small bowls, sprinkle the cilantro on top and serve.

Nutrition:
- Calories 123,
- Fat 4g,
- Fiber 1g,
- Carbs 3g,
- Protein 5g

140. Blackberries Caprese Skewers

Level of difficulty: Novice level
Preparation Time: 15 Minutes
Cooking Time: 0 Minutes
Servings: 4

Ingredients:
- ½ cup cherry tomatoes
- Four fresh basil leaves
- Four blackberries
- ¼ cup baby mozzarella balls

Directions:
1. Put blackberries, tomatoes, mozzarella balls, and basil on skewers.
2. Once done, serve.

Nutrition:
- Calories 40
- Fat 1.7g
- Total carbs 4g
- Protein 2g

141. Yogurt Dip

Level of difficulty: Novice level
Preparation Time: 10 Minutes
Cooking Time: 0 Minutes
Servings: 6

Ingredients:
- 2 cups Greek yogurt
- Two tbsp. pistachios, toasted and chopped
- A pinch of salt and white pepper
- Two tbsp. mint, chopped
- One tbsp. kalamata olives, pitted and chopped
- ¼ cup zaatar spice
- ¼ cup pomegranate seeds
- 1/3 cup olive oil

Directions:
1. Mix the yogurt with the pistachios and the rest of the ingredients, whisk well, divide into small cups and serve with pita chips on the side.

Nutrition:
- Calories 294
- Fat 18g
- Carbohydrates 2g
- Protein 10g
- Sodium 593 mg

142. Tomato Bruschetta

Level of difficulty: Novice level
Preparation Time: 10 Minutes
Cooking Time: 10 Minutes
Servings: 6

Ingredients:
- One baguette, sliced
- 1/3 cup basil, chopped
- Six tomatoes, cubed
- Two garlic cloves, minced
- A pinch of salt and black pepper
- One teaspoon olive oil
- One tbsp. balsamic vinegar
- ½ teaspoon garlic powder
- Cooking spray

Directions:

1. Situate the baguette slices on a baking sheet lined with parchment paper, grease with cooking spray. Bake for 10 minutes at 400 degrees.
2. Blend the tomatoes with the basil and the remaining ingredients, toss well and leave aside for 10 minutes. Divide the tomato mix on each baguette slice, arrange them all on a platter and serve.

Nutrition:
- Calories 162
- Fat 4g
- Carbohydrates 29g
- Protein 4g
- Sodium 736mg

143. Pepper Tapenade

Level of difficulty: Novice level
Preparation Time: 10 Minutes
Cooking Time: 0 Minutes
Servings: 4
Ingredients:
- 7 ounces roasted red peppers, chopped
- ½ cup parmesan, grated
- 1/3 cup parsley, chopped
- 14 ounces canned artichokes, drained and chopped
- Three tbsp. olive oil
- ¼ cup capers, drained
- One and ½ tbsp. lemon juice
- Two garlic cloves, minced

Directions:
In your blender, combine the red peppers with the parmesan and the rest of the ingredients and pulse well. Divide into cups and serve as a snack.

Nutrition:
- Calories 200
- Fat 5.6g
- Carbohydrates 12.4g
- Protein 4.6g
- Sodium 736 mg

144. Red Pepper Hummus

Level of difficulty: Novice level
Preparation Time: 10 Minutes
Cooking Time: 0 Minutes
Servings: 6
Ingredients:
- 6 ounces roasted red peppers, peeled and chopped
- 16 ounces canned chickpeas, drained and rinsed
- ¼ cup Greek yogurt
- Three tbsp. tahini paste
- Juice of 1 lemon
- Three garlic cloves, minced
- One tbsp. olive oil
- A pinch of salt and black pepper
- One tbsp. parsley, chopped

Directions:
1. In your food processor, combine the red peppers with the rest of the ingredients. Do not include the oil and the parsley and pulse well.
2. Add the oil, pulse again, divide into cups, sprinkle the parsley on top, and serve as a party spread.

Nutrition:
- Calories 255
- Fat 11.4g
- Carbohydrates 17.4g
- Protein 6.5mg
- Sodium 593 mg

145. Cucumber Bites

Level of difficulty: Novice level
Preparation Time: 10 minutes
Cooking Time: 0 minutes
Servings: 12
Ingredients:

- 1 English cucumber, sliced into 32 rounds
- 10 oz. hummus
- 16 cherry tomatoes, halved
- 1 tbsp. parsley, chopped
- 1 oz. feta cheese, crumbled

Directions:
1. Spread the hummus on each cucumber round, divide the tomato halves on each, sprinkle the cheese and parsley on to and serve as an appetizer.

Nutrition:
- Calories 162;
- Fat 3.4 g;
- Carbs 6.4 g;
- Protein 2.4 g

146. Stuffed Avocado

Level of difficulty: Intermediate
Preparation Time: 10 minutes
Cooking Time: 0 minute
Servings: 2
Ingredients:
- 1 avocado, halved and pitted
- 10 oz. canned tuna, drained
- 2 tbsp. sun-dried tomatoes, chopped
- 1 and ½ tbsp. basil pesto
- 2 tbsp. black olives, pitted and chopped
- Salt and black pepper to the taste
- 2 tsp. pine nuts, toasted and chopped
- 1 tbsp. basil, chopped

Directions:
1. In a bowl, combine the tuna with the sun-dried tomatoes and the rest of the ingredients except the avocado and stir.
2. Stuff the avocado halves with the tuna mix and serve as an appetizer.

Nutrition:
- Calories 233;
- Fat 9 g;
- Carbs 11.4 g;
- Protein 5.6 g

147. Hummus with Ground Lamb

Level of difficulty: Novice level
Preparation Time: 10 minutes
Cooking Time: 15 minutes
Servings: 8
Ingredients:
- 10 oz. hummus
- 12 oz. lamb meat, ground
- ½ cup pomegranate seeds
- ¼ cup parsley, chopped
- 1 tbsp. olive oil
- Pita chips for serving

Directions:
1. Heat up a pan with the oil over medium-high heat, add the meat, and brown for 15 minutes stirring often.
2. Spread the hummus on a platter, spread the ground lamb all over, also spread the pomegranate seeds and the parsley and serve with pita chips as a snack.

Nutrition:
- Calories 133;
- Fat 9.7 g;
- Carbs 6.4 g;
- Protein 5 g

148. Wrapped Plums

Level of difficulty: Novice level
Preparation Time: 5 minutes
Cooking Time: 0 minutes
Servings: 8
Ingredients:
- 2 oz. prosciutto, cut into 16 pieces
- 4 plums, quartered
- 1 tbsp. chives, chopped

- A pinch of red pepper flakes, crushed

Directions:
1. Wrap each plum quarter in a prosciutto slice, arrange them all on a platter, sprinkle the chives and pepper flakes all over and serve.

Nutrition:
- Calories 30;
- Fat 1 g;
- Carbs 4 g;
- Protein 2 g

149. Cucumber Sandwich Bites

Level of difficulty: Novice level
Preparation Time: 5 minutes
Cooking Time: 0 minutes
Servings: 12
Ingredients:
- 1 cucumber, sliced
- 8 slices whole wheat bread
- 2 tbsp. cream cheese, soft
- 1 tbsp. chives, chopped
- ¼ cup avocado, peeled, pitted and mashed
- 1 tsp. mustard
- Salt and black pepper to the taste

Directions:
1. Spread the mashed avocado on each bread slice, also spread the rest of the ingredients except the cucumber slices.
2. Divide the cucumber slices on the bread slices, cut each slice in thirds, arrange on a platter and serve as an appetizer.

Nutrition:
- Calories 187;
- Fat 12.4 g;
- Carbs 4.5 g;
- Protein 8.2 g

150. Cucumber Rolls

Level of difficulty: Novice level
Preparation Time: 5 minutes
Cooking Time: 0 minutes
Servings: 6
Ingredients:
- 1 big cucumber, sliced lengthwise
- 1 tbsp. parsley, chopped
- 8 oz. canned tuna, drained and mashed
- Salt and black pepper to the taste
- 1 tsp. lime juice

Directions:
1. Arrange cucumber slices on a working surface, divide the rest of the ingredients, and roll.
2. Arrange all the rolls on a platter and serve as an appetizer.

Nutrition:
- Calories 200;
- Fat 6 g;
- Carbs 7.6 g;
- Protein 3.5 g

151. Olives and Cheese Stuffed Tomatoes

Level of difficulty: Novice level
Preparation Time: 10 minutes
Cooking Time: 0 minutes
Servings: 24
Ingredients:
- 24 cherry tomatoes, top cut off and insides scooped out
- 2 tbsp. olive oil
- ¼ tsp. red pepper flakes
- ½ cup feta cheese, crumbled
- 2 tbsp. black olive paste
- ¼ cup mint, torn

Directions:
1. In a bowl, mix the olives paste with the rest of the ingredients except the cherry tomatoes and whisk well. Stuff the

cherry tomatoes with this mix, arrange them all on a platter and serve as an appetizer.

Nutrition:
- Calories 136;
- Fat 8.6 g;
- Carbs 5.6 g;
- Protein 5.1 g

152. Tomato Salsa

Level of difficulty: Novice level
Preparation Time: 5 minutes
Cooking Time: 0 minutes
Servings: 6
Ingredients:
- 1 garlic clove, minced
- 4 tbsp. olive oil
- 5 tomatoes, cubed
- 1 tbsp. balsamic vinegar
- ¼ cup basil, chopped
- 1 tbsp. parsley, chopped
- 1 tbsp. chives, chopped
- Salt and black pepper to the taste
- Pita chips for serving

Directions:
1. In a bowl, mix the tomatoes with the garlic and the rest of the ingredients except the pita chips, stir, divide into small cups and serve with the pita chips on the side.

Nutrition:
- Calories 160;
- Fat 13.7 g;
- Carbs 10.1 g;
- Protein 2.2 g

153. Chili Mango and Watermelon Salsa

Level of difficulty: Novice level
Preparation Time: 5 minutes
Cooking Time: 0 minutes
Servings: 12
Ingredients:
- 1 red tomato, chopped
- Salt and black pepper to the taste
- 1 cup watermelon, seedless, peeled and cubed
- 1 red onion, chopped
- 2 mangos, peeled and chopped
- 2 chili peppers, chopped
- ¼ cup cilantro, chopped
- 3 tbsp. lime juice
- Pita chips for serving

Directions:
1. In a bowl, mix the tomato with the watermelon, the onion and the rest of the ingredients except the pita chips and toss well. Divide the mix into small cups and serve with pita chips on the side.

Nutrition:
- Calories 62;
- Fat 2g;
- Fiber 1.3 g;
- Carbs 3.9 g;
- Protein 2.3 g

154. Creamy Spinach and Shallots Dip

Level of difficulty: Novice level
Preparation Time: 10 minutes
Cooking Time: 0 minutes
Servings: 4
Ingredients:
- 1 lb. spinach, roughly chopped
- 2 shallots, chopped
- 2 tbsp. mint, chopped
- ¾ cup cream cheese, soft
- Salt and black pepper to the taste

Directions:
1. In a blender, combine the spinach with the shallots and the rest of the

ingredients, and pulse well. Divide into small bowls and serve as a party dip.

Nutrition:
- Calories 204;
- Fat 11.5 g;
- Carbs 4.2 g;
- Protein 5.9 g

155. Feta Artichoke Dip

Level of difficulty: Intermediate
Preparation Time: 10 minutes
Cooking Time: 30 minutes
Servings: 8
Ingredients:
- 8 oz. artichoke hearts, drained and quartered
- ¾ cup basil, chopped
- ¾ cup green olives, pitted and chopped
- 1 cup parmesan cheese, grated
- 5 oz. feta cheese, crumbled

Directions:
1. In your food processor, mix the artichokes with the basil and the rest of the ingredients, pulse well, and transfer to a baking dish.
2. Introduce in the oven, bake at 375° F for 30 minutes and serve as a party dip.

Nutrition:
- Calories 186;
- Fat 12.4 g;
- Fiber 0.9 g;
- Carbs 2.6 g;
- Protein 1.5 g

156. Avocado Dip

Level of difficulty: Novice level
Preparation Time: 5 minutes
Cooking Time: 0 minutes
Servings: 8
Ingredients:
- ½ cup heavy cream
- 1 green chili pepper, chopped
- Salt and pepper to the taste
- 4 avocados, pitted, peeled and chopped
- 1 cup cilantro, chopped
- ¼ cup lime juice

Directions:
1. In a blender, combine the cream with the avocados and the rest of the ingredients and pulse well. Divide the mix into bowls and serve cold as a party dip.

Nutrition:
- Calories 200;
- Fat 14.5 g;
- Fiber 3.8 g;
- Carbs 8.1 g;
- Protein 7.6 g

157. Goat Cheese and Chives Spread

Level of difficulty: Novice level
Preparation Time: 10 minutes
Cooking Time: 0 minute
Servings: 4
Ingredients:
- 2 oz. goat cheese, crumbled
- ¾ cup sour cream
- 2 tbsp. chives, chopped
- 1 tbsp. lemon juice
- Salt and black pepper to the taste
- 2 tbsp. extra virgin olive oil

Directions:
1. In a bowl, mix the goat cheese with the cream and the rest of the ingredients and whisk really well. Keep in the fridge for 10 minutes and serve as a party spread.

Nutrition:

- Calories 220;
- Fat 11.5 g;
- Carbs 8.9 g;
- Protein 5.6 g

158. Stuffed Chicken

Level of difficulty: Novice level
Preparation Time: 10 minutes
Cooking Time: 30 minutes
Servings: 4
Ingredients:
- 4 chicken breasts, skinless, boneless and butterflied
- 1 oz. spring onions, chopped
- ½ lb. white mushrooms, sliced
- 1 tsp. hot paprika
- A pinch of salt and black pepper
- 1 cup tomato sauce

Directions:
1. Flatten chicken breasts with a meat mallet and place them on a plate.
2. In a bowl, mix the spring onions with the mushrooms, paprika, salt and pepper and stir well.
3. Divide this on each chicken breast half, roll them and secure with a toothpick.
4. Add the tomato sauce in the instant pot, put the chicken rolls inside as well, put the lid on and cook on High for 30 minutes.
5. Release the pressure naturally for 10 minutes, arrange the stuffed chicken breasts on a platter and serve.

Nutrition:
- Calories 221,
- Fat 12g,
- Carbs 6g,
- Protein 11g

159. Cinnamon Baby Back Ribs Platter

Level of difficulty: Novice level
Preparation Time: 10 minutes
Cooking Time: 40 minutes
Servings: 2
Ingredients:
- 1 rack baby back ribs
- 2 tsp. smoked paprika
- 2 tsp. chili powder
- A pinch of salt and black pepper
- 1 tsp. garlic powder
- 1 tsp. onion powder
- 1 tsp. cinnamon powder
- ½ tsp. cumin seeds
- A pinch of cayenne pepper
- 1 cup tomato sauce
- 3 garlic cloves, minced

Directions:
1. In your instant pot, combine the baby back ribs with the rest of the ingredients, put the lid on and cook on High for 30 minutes.
2. Release the pressure naturally for 10 minutes, arrange the ribs on a platter and serve as an appetizer.

Nutrition:
- Calories 222,
- Fat 12g,
- Fiber 4g,
- Carbs 6g,

Protein 14g

160. Buttery Carrot Sticks

Level of difficulty: Novice level
Preparation Time: 10 minutes
Cooking Time: 15 minutes
Servings: 4
Ingredients:
- 1 lb. carrot, cut into sticks
- 4 garlic cloves, minced

- ¼ cup chicken stock
- 1 tsp. rosemary, chopped
- A pinch of salt and black pepper
- 2 tbsp. olive oil
- 2 tbsp. ghee, melted

Directions:
1. Set the instant pot on Sauté mode, add the oil and the ghee, heat them up, add the garlic and brown for 1 minute.
2. Add the rest of the ingredients, put the lid on and cook on High for 14 minutes.
3. Release the pressure naturally for 10 minutes, arrange the carrot sticks on a platter and serve.

Nutrition:
- Calories 142,
- Fat 4g,
- Carbs 5g,
- Protein 7

CHAPTER 6. DESERTS

161. Maple Vanilla Baked Pears

Level of difficulty: Novice level
Preparation Time: 10 minutes
Cooking Time: 30 minutes
Servings: 4
Ingredients:
- 4 D'Anjou pears
- Pure Maple Syrup 1/2 cup (120ml)
- Ground cinnamon 1/4 teaspoon
- 1 teaspoon of pure vanilla extract
- Optional toppings: Greek yogurt, maple pecan granola

Directions:
2. Preheat the oven to 190°C (375°F).
3. Cut the pears, and cut a small sliver from the underside so that when set upright on the baking sheet, the pears sit flat. Core out the seeds using a big or medium cookie scoop and melon scoop (or even a teaspoon). Arrange the pears on the baking dish, face up. Sprinkle with cinnamon uniformly- if you like, feel free to add more cinnamon.
4. In a small bowl, mix the maple syrup and vanilla extract. Drizzle much of it all over the
5. Pears, reserving only 2 tbsp. for baking after the pears are completed.
6. Bake the pears for about 25 minutes, until the sides are soft and lightly browned. Remove from the oven and drizzle instantly with any leftover mixture of maple syrup. With the granola and yogurt, serve warm. Store the leftovers for up to 5 days in the refrigerator.

Nutrition:
- Kcal 153,
- Fat: 6g,
- Net Carbs: 16g,
- Protein: 6g

162. Easy roasted fruit recipe

Level of difficulty: Novice level
Preparation Time: 10 minutes
Cooking Time: 30 minutes
Servings: 4
Ingredients:
- Peaches 4, peeled & sliced
- Fresh blueberries 1 1/2 cups

- Ground cinnamon 1/8 teaspoon
- 3 tbsp. of brown sugar

Directions:
1. Preheat the oven to 350°F.
2. In a baking dish, spread the sliced peaches & blueberries. Sprinkled with brown sugar and cinnamon.
3. Bake for about 20 minutes at 350 degrees F, then change the oven settings to a low grill and broil for about five min, or until sparkling.
4. Serve warm, cover and refrigerate, or let cool.

Nutrition:
- Kcal 256,
- Fat: 9g,
- Net Carbs: 25g,
- Protein: 4g

163. Triple Chocolate Tiramisu

Level of difficulty: Intermediate
Preparation Time: 10 minutes
Cooking Time: 6 hours
Servings: 12
Ingredients:
- 2 3-ounce ladyfingers package, split
- 1/4 cup of espresso brewed or strong coffee
- 1 8 ounces mascarpone carton cheese
- 1 cup of whipped cream
- 1/4 cup of sugar powdered
- 1 teaspoon of vanilla
- 1/3 cup of chocolate liqueur
- White baking bars of 1 ounce, grated
- 1 ounce bittersweet, grated chocolate
- Unsweetened cocoa powdered
- Chopped coffee beans covered in chocolate (optional)

Directions:
1. With some of the ladyfingers, line the bottom of an 8x8x2-inch baking pan, cutting to fit as required. Drizzle over the ladyfingers with half of the espresso; set aside.
2. Beat together the mascarpone cheese, powdered sugar, whipped cream, and vanilla with an electric mixer in a medium mixing cup, only before stiff peaks develop. Up until now combined, beat in the chocolate liqueur. Spoon half of the mascarpone combination, pouring evenly around the ladyfingers. Sprinkle over the mascarpone mixture of white chocolate and bittersweet chocolate. Top with a different layer of ladyfinger (reserve any leftover ladyfingers for another use). A layer with the remaining mixture of espresso and mascarpone cheese.
3. For 6 to 24 hours, cover and chill. Sift the cocoa powder over the dessert top. Garnish with cocoa beans, if desired.
4. Make twelve squares.

Nutrition:
- Kcal 256,
- Fat: 19g,
- Net Carbs: 17g,
- Protein: 6g

164. Easy Strawberry Crepes Recipe

Level of difficulty: Novice level
Preparation Time: 10 minutes
Cooking Time: 12 minutes
Servings: 12
Ingredients:

- 2 cups of sliced frozen strawberries, thawed
- 2 tbsp. of sugar
- Orange zest 1/2 teaspoon, optional
- 3 cups of fresh strawberries, diced
- Large eggs 2
- 2 tbsp. butter, slightly melted and cooled
- 2 cups of milk
- 1 teaspoon of vanilla
- 1 tbsp. of sugar
- 1/2 tsp of salt
- 1 1/2 cups flour

Directions:
For Strawberry filling
1. Gently puree the strawberries to thaw. Stir in honey, orange zest if using, and fresh sliced strawberries. Serve at room temperature with a strawberry filling.

For Crêpes
2. In the order listed, add the ingredients to the blender jar, cover and blend until smooth.
3. Until cooking, refrigerate overnight or for 1 hour. (Or you can strain any lumps and use them immediately if you'd prefer.)
4. Over medium heat, heat the crepe pan or an 8-inch skillet and brush loosely with butter or cooking spray. Pour 1/4 cup of batter into the middle of the skillet with each crepe and then roll the pan, so the batter covers the skillet's bottom with a thin layer. Cook for about 1 minute, before light brown and the top, starts to dry out. Flip and boil for an extra 30 seconds.
5. Repeat for the batter that remains. Pile the completed crepes on a tray. (Place wax paper between the crepes if the crepes hold together.) In a 200 degrees C oven, you should put crepes to stay warm before ready to serve.
6. With a strawberry filling, fill each crepe and roll-up. With whipped cream, serve it.

Nutrition:
- Kcal 120,
- Fat: 7g,
- Net Carbs: 18g,
- Protein: 6g

165. Dried Fruit Compote

Level of difficulty: Novice level
Preparation Time: 5 minutes
Cooking Time: 20 minutes
Servings: 6
Ingredients:

- 8 ounces dried apricots, quartered
- 8 ounces dried peaches, quartered
- 1 cup golden raisins
- 1½ cups orange juice

- 1 cinnamon stick
- 4 whole cloves

Directions:
1. Stir to merge. Close, select the Manual button, and adjust the time to 3 minutes. When the timer beeps, let pressure release naturally, about 20 minutes. Press the Cancel button and open lid.
2. Remove and discard cinnamon stick and cloves. Press the Sauté button and simmer for 5–6 minutes. Serve warm then cover and refrigerate for up to a week.

Nutrition:
- 258 Calories
- 5g Fat
- 8g Carbohydrates
- 4g Protein

166. Chocolate Rice Pudding

Level of difficulty: Novice level
Preparation Time: 10 minutes
Cooking Time: 20 minutes
Servings: 6
Ingredients:
- 2 cups almond milk
- 1 cup long-grain brown rice
- 2 tbsp. Dutch-processed cocoa powder
- ¼ cup maple syrup
- 1 teaspoon vanilla extract
- ½ cup chopped dark chocolate

Directions:
1. Place almond milk, rice, cocoa, maple syrup, and vanilla in the Instant Pot®. Close then select the Manual button, and set time to 20 minutes.
2. When the timer beeps, let pressure release naturally for 15 minutes, then quick-release the remaining pressure. Press the Cancel button and open lid. Serve warm, sprinkled with chocolate.

Nutrition:
- 271 Calories
- 8g Fat
- 4g Carbohydrates
- 3g Protein

167. Fruit Compote

Level of difficulty: Intermediate
Preparation Time: 10 minutes
Cooking Time: 15 minutes
Servings: 6
Ingredients:
- 1 cup apple juice
- 1 cup dry white wine
- 2 tbsp. honey
- 1 cinnamon stick
- ¼ teaspoon ground nutmeg
- 1 tbsp. grated lemon zest
- 1½ tbsp. grated orange zest
- 3 large apples, peeled, cored, and chopped
- 3 large pears, peeled, cored, and chopped
- ½ cup dried cherries

Directions:
1. Situate all ingredients in the Instant Pot® and stir well. Close and select the Manual button, and allow to sit for 1 minute. When the timer beeps, rapidly-release the pressure until the float valve hit the bottom. Click the Cancel then open lid.
2. Use a slotted spoon to transfer fruit to a serving bowl. Remove and discard cinnamon stick. Press the Sauté button and bring juice in the pot to a boil. Cook, stirring constantly, until reduced to a syrup that will coat the back of a spoon, about 10 minutes.

3. Stir syrup into fruit mixture. Once cool slightly, then wrap with plastic and chill overnight.

Nutrition:
- 211 Calories
- 1g Fat
- 4g Carbohydrates
- 2g Protein

168. Stuffed Apples

Level of difficulty: Novice level
Preparation Time: 10 minutes
Cooking Time: 15 minutes
Servings: 6
Ingredients:
- ½ cup apple juice
- ¼ cup golden raisins
- ¼ cup chopped toasted walnuts
- 2 tbsp. sugar
- ½ teaspoon grated orange zest
- ½ teaspoon ground cinnamon
- 4 large cooking apples
- 4 teaspoons unsalted butter
- 1 cup water

Directions:
1. Put apple juice in a microwave-safe container; heat for 1 minute on high or until steaming and hot. Pour over raisins. Soak raisins for 30 minutes. Drain, reserving apple juice. Add nuts, sugar, orange zest, and cinnamon to raisins and stir to mix.
2. Cut off the top fourth of each apple. Peel the cut portion and chop it, then stir diced apple pieces into raisin mixture. Hollow out and core apples by cutting to, but not through, the bottoms.
3. Situate each apple on a piece of aluminum foil that is large enough to wrap apple completely. Fill apple centers with raisin mixture.
4. Top each with 1 teaspoon butter. Cover the foil around each apple, folding the foil over at the top and then pinching it firmly together.
5. Stir in water to the Instant Pot® and place rack inside. Place apples on the rack. Close lid, set steam release to Sealing, press the Manual, and alarm to 10 minutes.
6. When the timer beeps, quick-release the pressure until the float valve drops and open the lid. Carefully lift apples out of the Instant Pot®. Unwrap and transfer to plates. Serve hot, at room temperature, or cold.

Nutrition:
- 432 Calories
- 16g Fat
- 6g Carbohydrates
- 3g Protein

169. Cinnamon-Stewed Dried Plums with Greek Yogurt

Level of difficulty: Novice level
Preparation Time: 10 minutes
Cooking Time: 15 minutes
Servings: 6
Ingredients:
- 3 cups dried plums
- 2 cups water
- 2 tbsp. sugar
- 2 cinnamon sticks
- 3 cups low-fat plain Greek yogurt

Directions:
1. Add dried plums, water, sugar, and cinnamon to the Instant Pot®. Close allow steam release to Sealing, press the Manual button, and start the time to 3 minutes.

2. Once the timer beeps, quick-release the pressure. Click the Cancel button and open. Remove and discard cinnamon sticks. Serve warm over Greek yogurt.

Nutrition:
- 301 Calories
- 2g Fat
- 3g Carbohydrates
- 14g Protein

170. Vanilla-Poached Apricots

Level of difficulty: Novice level
Preparation Time: 10 minutes
Cooking Time: 20 minutes
Servings: 6
Ingredients:
- 1¼ cups water
- ¼ cup marsala wine
- ¼ cup sugar
- 1 teaspoon vanilla bean paste
- 8 medium apricots, sliced in half and pitted

Directions:
1. Place all pieces in the Instant Pot® and combine well. Seal tight, click the Manual Instant Pot®. Stir to combine. Close lid, set steam release to Sealing, press the Manual button, and set second to 1 minute.
2. When the alarm beeps, quick-release the pressure until the float valve drops. Set the Cancel and open lid. Let stand for 10 minutes. Carefully remove apricots from poaching liquid with a slotted spoon. Serve warm or at room temperature.

Nutrition:
- 62 Calories
- 1g Fat
- 5g Carbohydrates
- 2g Protein

171. Creamy Spiced Almond Milk

Level of difficulty: Novice level
Preparation Time: 10 minutes
Cooking Time: 15 minutes
Servings: 6
Ingredients:
- 1 cup raw almonds
- 5 cups filtered water, divided
- 1 teaspoon vanilla bean paste
- ½ teaspoon pumpkin pie spice

Directions:
1. Stir in almonds and 1 cup water to the Instant Pot®. Close and select the Manual, and set time to 1 minute.
2. When the timer alarms, quick-release the pressure until the float valve drops. Click the Cancel button and open cap. Strain almonds and rinse under cool water. Transfer to a high-powered blender with remaining 4 cups water. Purée for 2 minutes on high speed.
3. Incorporate mixture into a nut milk bag set over a large bowl. Squeeze bag to extract all liquid. Stir in vanilla and pumpkin pie spice. Transfer to a Mason jar or sealed jug and refrigerate for 8 hours. Stir or shake gently before serving.

Nutrition:
- 86 Calories
- 8g Fat
- 5g Carbohydrates
- 3g Protein

172. Poached Pears with Greek Yogurt and Pistachio

Level of difficulty: Novice level
Preparation Time: 10 minutes
Cooking Time: 15 minutes
Servings: 8
Ingredients:

- 2 cups water
- 1¾ cups apple cider
- ¼ cup lemon juice
- 1 cinnamon stick
- 1 teaspoon vanilla bean paste
- 4 large Bartlett pears, peeled
- 1 cup low-fat plain Greek yogurt
- ½ cup unsalted roasted pistachio meats

Directions:
1. Add water, apple cider, lemon juice, cinnamon, vanilla, and pears to the Instant Pot®. Close lid, set steam release, switch the Manual, and set time to 3 minutes.
2. When the timer stops, swift-release the pressure until the float valve drops. Select the Cancel button and open cap. Take out pears to a plate and allow to cool to room temperature.
3. To serve, carefully slice pears in half with a sharp paring knife and scoop out core with a melon baller. Lay pear halves on dessert plates or in shallow bowls. Top with yogurt and garnish with pistachios. Serve immediately.

Nutrition:
- 181 Calories
- 7g Fat
- 5g Carbohydrates
- 7g Protein

173. Peaches Poached in Rose Water

Level of difficulty: Novice level
Preparation Time: 10 minutes
Cooking Time: 20 minutes
Servings: 6
Ingredients:
- 1 cup water
- 1 cup rose water
- ¼ cup wildflower honey
- 8 green cardamom pods, lightly crushed
- 1 teaspoon vanilla bean paste
- 6 large yellow peaches, pitted and quartered
- ½ cup chopped unsalted roasted pistachio meats

Directions:
1. Add water, rose water, honey, cardamom, and vanilla to the Instant Pot®. Whisk well, then add peaches. Close lid, allow to steam release to Seal, press the Manual button, and alarm time to 1 minute.
2. When done, release the pressure until the float valve hits the bottom. Press the Remove and open it. Allow peaches to stand for 10 minutes. Carefully remove peaches from poaching liquid with a slotted spoon.
3. Slip skins from peach slices. Arrange slices on a plate and garnish with pistachios. Serve warm or at room temperature.

Nutrition:
- 145 Calories
- 3g Fat
- 6g Carbohydrates
- 2g Protein

174. Brown Betty Apple Dessert

Level of difficulty: Novice level
Preparation Time: 10 minutes
Cooking Time: 10 minutes
Servings: 8
Ingredients:
- 2 cups dried bread crumbs
- ½ cup sugar
- 1 teaspoon ground cinnamon
- 3 tbsp. lemon juice

- 1 tbsp. grated lemon zest
- 1 cup olive oil, divided
- 8 medium apples, peeled, cored, and diced
- 2 cups water

Directions:
1. Combine crumbs, sugar, cinnamon, lemon juice, lemon zest, and ½ cup oil in a medium mixing bowl. Set aside.
2. In a greased oven-safe dish that will fit in your cooker loosely, add a thin layer of crumbs, then one diced apple. Continue filling the container with alternating layers of crumbs and apples until all ingredients are finished. Pour remaining ½ cup oil on top.
3. Pour water to the Instant Pot® and place rack inside. Make a foil sling by folding a long piece of foil in half lengthwise and lower the uncovered container into the pot using the sling.
4. Seal and press the Manual button, and set time to 10 minutes. When the timer stops, let pressure release naturally, about 20 minutes. Press the Cancel button and open lid. Using the sling, remove the baking dish from the pot and let stand for 5 minutes before serving.

Nutrition:
- 422 Calories
- 27g Fat
- 4g Carbohydrates
- 7g Protein

175. Blueberry Oat Crumble

Level of difficulty: Novice level
Preparation Time: 10 minutes
Cooking Time: 10 minutes
Servings: 8
Ingredients:
- 1 cup water
- 4 cups blueberries
- 2 tbsp. packed light brown sugar
- 2 tbsp. cornstarch
- 1/8 teaspoon ground nutmeg
- 1/3 cup rolled oats
- ¼ cup granulated sugar
- ¼ cup all-purpose flour
- ¼ teaspoon ground cinnamon
- ¼ cup unsalted butter, melted and cooled

Directions:
1. Brush baking dish that fits inside the Instant Pot® with nonstick cooking spray. Add water to the pot and add rack. Crease a long piece of aluminum foil in half lengthwise. Lay foil over rack to form a sling.
2. In a medium bowl, combine blueberries, brown sugar, cornstarch, and nutmeg. Transfer mixture to prepared dish.
3. In a separate medium bowl, add oats, sugar, flour, and cinnamon. Mix well. Add butter and combine until mixture is crumbly. Sprinkle crumbles over blueberries, cover dish with aluminum foil, and crimp edges tightly.
4. Add baking dish to rack in pot so it rests on the sling and seal tight. Switch the Manual button, and set time to 10 minutes. When the timer beeps, let pressure release naturally for 10 minutes, then quick-release the remaining pressure until the float valve drops. Press the Cancel button and open lid. Carefully remove dish with sling and remove foil cover.
5. Heat broiler on high. Broil crumble until topping is golden brown, about 5 minutes. Serve warm or at room temperature.

Nutrition:
- 159 Calories
- 6g Fat
- 3g Carbohydrates
- 2g Protein

176. Date and Walnut Cookies

Level of difficulty: Intermediate
Preparation Time: 10 minutes
Cooking Time: 2 minutes
Servings: 30
Ingredients:
- 2 cups flour
- 1/4 cup sour cream
- 1/2 cup butter, softened
- 1 1/2 cups brown sugar
- 1/2 cup white sugar
- 1 egg
- 1 cup dates, pitted and chopped
- 1/3 cup water
- 1/4 cup walnuts, finely chopped
- 1/2 tsp salt
- 1/2 tsp baking soda
- a pinch of cinnamon

Directions:
1. Cook the dates together with the white sugar and water over medium-high heat, stirring constantly, until mixture is thick like jam. Add in the nuts, stir and remove from heat. Leave to cool.
2. In a medium bowl, scourge the butter and brown sugar. Stir in the egg and the sour cream. Mix the flour together with salt, baking soda and cinnamon and stir it into the butter mixture.
3. Drop a teaspoon of dough onto a cookie sheet, place 1/4 teaspoon of the filling on top of it and top with an additional 1/2 teaspoon of dough. Repeat with the rest of the dough. Bake cookies for about 10 minutes in a preheated to 340 F oven, or until golden.

Nutrition:
- 134 Calories
- 7.9g Fats
- 2g Carbohydrates
- 1.4g Protein

177. Moroccan Stuffed Dates

Level of difficulty: Novice level
Preparation Time: 15 minutes
Cooking Time: 0 minute
Servings: 30
Ingredients:
- 1 lb. dates
- 1 cup blanched almonds
- 1/4 cup sugar
- 1 1/2 tbsp. orange flower water
- 1 tbsp. butter, melted
- 1/4 teaspoon cinnamon

Directions:
1. Incorporate the almonds, sugar and cinnamon in a food processor. Stir in the butter and orange flower water and process until a smooth paste is formed. Roll small pieces of almond paste the same length as a date.
2. Take one date, make a vertical cut and discard the pit. Insert a piece of the almond paste and press the sides of the date firmly around. Repeat with all the remaining dates and almond paste.

Nutrition:
- 102 Calories
- 7g Fats
- 5g Carbohydrates
- 2g Protein

178. Fig Cookies

Level of difficulty: Novice level
Preparation Time: 10 minutes

Cooking Time: 15 minutes
Servings: 24
Ingredients:
- 1 cup flour
- 1 egg
- 1/2 cup sugar
- 1/2 cup figs, chopped
- 1/2 cup butter
- 1/4 cup water
- 1/2 tsp vanilla extract
- 1 tsp baking powder
- a pinch of salt

Directions:
1. Cook figs with water, stirring, for 4-5 minutes, or until thickened. Set aside to cool. Scourge butter with sugar until light and fluffy. Put in the egg and vanilla and beat to blend well. In separate bowl, incorporate together flour, baking powder and salt. Blend this into the egg mixture. Stir in the cooled figs.
2. Drop teaspoonful of dough on a greased baking tray. Bake in a preheated to 375 degrees F oven until lightly browned. Remove cookies and cool on wire racks.

Nutrition:
- 111 Calories
- 9g Fats
- 5g Carbohydrates
- 3g Protein

179. Turkish delight Cookies

Level of difficulty: Novice level
Preparation Time: 5 minutes
Cooking Time: 20 minutes
Servings: 48
Ingredients:
- 4 cups flour
- 3/4 cup sugar
- 1 cup lard (or butter)
- 3 eggs
- 1 tsp baking powder
- 1 tsp vanilla extract
- 8 oz. Turkish delight, chopped
- powdered sugar, for dusting

Directions:
1. Ready oven to 375 F. Put parchment paper onto the baking sheet. Beat the eggs well, adding sugar a bit at a time. Beat for at least 3 minutes. Melt the lard, then let it cool enough and slowly combine it with the egg mixture.
2. Mix the flour and the baking powder. Lightly add the flour mixture to the egg and lard mixture to create a smooth dough. Divide dough into two or three smaller balls and roll it out until ¼ inch thick. Cut squares 3x2 inch. Situate a piece of Turkish delight in each square, roll each cookie into a stick and nip the end. Bake in a preheated to 350 degrees F oven until light pink. Dust in powdered sugar and store in an airtight container when completely cool.

Nutrition:
- 109 Calories
- 7g Fats
- 5g Carbohydrates
- 3g Protein

180. Anise Cookies

Level of difficulty: Novice level
Preparation Time: 10 minutes
Cooking Time: 20 minutes
Servings: 24
Ingredients:
- 1 ½ cups flour
- 1/3 cup sugar
- 1/3 cup olive oil
- 1 egg, whisked

- 3 tsp fennel seeds
- 1 tsp cinnamon
- zest of one orange
- 3 tbsp. anise liqueur
- sugar, for sprinkling

Directions:
1. Cook olive oil in a small pan and sauté fennel seeds for 20-30 seconds. In a large bowl, combine together flour, sugar, and cinnamon. Add in olive oil, stirring, until well combined. Add orange zest and anise liqueur. Mix well then knead with hands until a smooth dough is formed. Add a little water if necessary.
2. On a well-floured surface, form two 1-inch-long logs. Cut 1/8-inch cookies, arrange them on greased baking sheets. Egg washes each cookie and sprinkle with sugar. Bake cookies in a preheated to 350 F oven, for about 10 minutes, or until golden and crisp. Once cool, put in an airtight container.

Nutrition:
- 113 Calories
- 8g Fats
- 5g Carbohydrates
- 2g Protein

181. Spanish Nougat

Level of difficulty: Novice level
Preparation Time: 5 minutes
Cooking Time: 20 minutes
Servings: 24
Ingredients:
- 1 1/2 cup honey
- 3 egg whites
- 1 ¾ cup almonds, roasted and chopped

Directions:
1. Put the honey into a saucepan and boil over medium-high heat, then set aside to cool. Beat the egg whites to a thick glossy meringue and fold them into the honey. Bring the mixture back to medium-high heat and let it simmer, constantly stirring, for 15 minutes. When the color and consistency change to dark caramel, remove from heat, add the almonds and mix trough.
2. Put foil in a 9x13 inch pan and pour the hot mixture on it. Cover with another piece of foil and even out. Let cool completely. Place a wooden board weighted down with some heavy cans on it. Leave like this for 3-4 days, so it hardens and dries out. Slice into 1-inch squares.

Nutrition:
- 110 Calories
- 5g Fats
- 7g Carbohydrates
- 1g Protein

182. Spanish Crumble Cakes

Level of difficulty: Novice level
Preparation Time: 10 minutes
Cooking Time: 25 minutes
Servings: 30
Ingredients:
- 2 cups flour
- 1 cup butter, softened
- 1 cup sugar
- 1 egg
- 1 tsp lemon zest
- 1 tsp orange zest
- 1 tbsp. orange juice
- 1/2 cup almonds, blanched and finely ground

Directions:
1. Beat butter with sugar, lemon and orange zest until light. Combine in the flour, using a wooden spoon. Add ground almonds, stir, then knead with your hands until dough clings together.

Divide it in three parts. Seal and chill for at least half an hour.
2. On a well-floured surface, roll out each piece of dough until it is 1/4 inch thick. Cut into different shapes. Arrange cookies on an ungreased baking sheet.
3. Beat together egg and orange juice and brush this over the cookies. Bake in a preheated to 350 degrees F oven for 7-8 minutes, or until edges are lightly golden. Set aside and keep in an airtight container.

Nutrition:
- 113 Calories
- 8g Fats
- 5g Carbohydrates
- 4g Protein

183. Greek Honey Cookies

Level of difficulty: Novice level
Preparation Time: 10 minutes
Cooking Time: 15 minutes
Servings: 40
Ingredients:
- 1 ¾ cups olive oil
- 2 cups walnuts, coarsely ground
- 1 cup sugar
- 1 cup fresh orange juice
- 3 tbsp. orange peel
- 1/3 cup cognac
- 1 ½ tsp baking soda
- 1 tsp baking powder
- sifted flour, enough to make soft oily dough

For the syrup
- 2 cups honey
- 1 cup water

For sprinkling
- 1 cup very finely ground walnuts
- 1 tsp ground cinnamon
- 1 tsp ground cloves

Directions:
1. Line 2 baking trays with baking paper. In a very large bowl, scourge together oil, sugar, orange zest, orange juice, cognac, baking soda, baking powder, and salt until well combined. Fold in flour with a wooden spoon until a soft dough is formed.
2. Roll tablespoonsful of the mixture into balls. Place them, about 1.5 inch apart, on the prepared trays. With a fork to prick the top of each cookie by cross-pressing. Bake in a preheated to 350 degrees F oven, for 30-35 minutes, or until golden.
3. Situate the water and honey in a medium saucepan over medium-high heat. Simmer for 5 minutes, removing foam. Set heat to low and with the help of a perforated spoon, dip 5-6 cookies at a time into the syrup. Once the cookies have absorbed a little of the syrup, remove them with the same spoon and situate them on a tray to cool and get rid of any excess syrup. After dipping the cookies, sprinkle with a mixture of cinnamon, cloves and finely ground walnuts.

Nutrition:
- 116 Calories
- 7g Fats
- 6g Carbohydrates
- 2g Protein

184. Cinnamon Butter Cookies

Level of difficulty: Novice level
Preparation Time: 10 minutes
Cooking Time: 20 minutes
Servings: 24
Ingredients:
- 2 cups flour
- 1/2 cup sugar

- 5 tbsp. butter
- 3 eggs
- 1 tbsp. cinnamon

Directions:
1. Scourge the butter and sugar until light and fluffy. Combine the flour and the cinnamon. Beat eggs into the butter mixture. Gently add in the flour. Situate the dough onto a lightly floured surface and knead just once or twice until smooth.
2. Form a roll and divide it into 24 pieces. Grease and line baking sheets with parchment paper. Spread each piece of cookie dough into a long thin strip, then make a circle, flatten a little and set it on the prepared baking sheet. Bake cookies, in batches, in a preheated to 350 F oven, for 12 to 15 minutes. Set aside in a cooling rack.

Nutrition:
- 111 Calories
- 5g Fats
- 3g Carbohydrates
- 9g Protein

185. Best French Meringues

Level of difficulty: Novice level
Preparation Time: 10 minutes
Cooking Time: 2 hours and 30 minutes
Servings: 36
Ingredients:
- 4 egg whites
- 2 1/4 cups powdered sugar

Directions:
1. Ready the oven to 200 F and line a baking sheet.
2. In a glass bowl, beat egg whites with an electric mixer. Mix in sugar a little simultaneously, while continuing to beat at medium speed. When the egg white mixture becomes stiff and shiny like satin, transfer to a large pastry bag. Place the meringue onto the lined baking sheet with the use of a large round.
3. Put the meringues in the oven and leave the oven door slightly ajar. Bake until the meringues are dry.

Nutrition:
- 110 Calories
- 11g Fat
- 6g Carbohydrates
- 3g Protein

186. Cinnamon Palmier

Level of difficulty: Intermediate
Preparation Time: 5 minutes
Cooking Time: 15 minutes
Servings: 30
Ingredients:
- 1/3 cup granulated sugar
- 2 tsp cinnamon
- 1/2 lb. puff pastry
- 1 egg, beaten (optional)

Directions:
1. Stir together the sugar and cinnamon. Spread the pastry dough into a large rectangle. Spread the cinnamon sugar in an even layer over the dough. From the long ends of the rectangle, loosely roll each side inward until they meet in the middle.
2. If needed, brush it with the egg to hold it together. Slice the pastry roll crosswise into 1/4-inch pieces and arrange them on a lined with parchment paper baking sheet. Bake cookies in a preheated to 400 F oven for 12-15 minutes, until they puff and turn golden brown. Serve warm or at room temperature.

Nutrition:
- 114 Calories
- 3g Fats
- 8g Carbohydrates
- 6g Protein

187. Honey Sesame Cookies

Level of difficulty: Novice level
Preparation Time: 10minutes
Cooking Time: 15 minutes
Servings: 30
Ingredients:
- 3 cups flour
- 1 cup sugar
- 1 cup butter
- 2 eggs
- 3 tbsp. honey
- 1 cup pistachio nuts, roughly chopped
- 1 cup sesame seeds
- 1 tbsp. vinegar
- 1 tsp vanilla
- 1 tsp baking powder
- a pinch of salt

Directions:
1. Scourge the butter and the sugar until light and fluffy. Gently add in the eggs, then the vanilla extract and the vinegar. Incorporate the flour, salt, and baking powder and stir in the butter mixture. Beat until just incorporated. Cover and refrigerate for an hour.
2. Mix the sesame seeds and the honey in a medium plate. Place the pistachios in another one. Take a teaspoonful of dough, form it into a ball, then dip it into the pistachios. Press a little and dip it into the sesame-honey mixture. Repeat with the remaining dough, arranging the cookies on a lined baking sheet.
3. Bake the cookies in a preheated to 350 F oven for 15 minutes, or until they turn light brown. Set aside in the baking sheet for 2-3 minutes then move to a wire rack.

Nutrition:
- 117 Calories
- 9g Fats
- 7g Carbohydrates
- 1g Protein

188. Baked Apples

Level of difficulty: Novice level
Preparation Time: 5 minutes
Cooking Time: 10 minutes
Servings: 4
Ingredients:
- 8 medium sized apples
- 1/3 cup walnuts, crushed
- 3/4 cup sugar
- 3 tbsp. raisins, soaked in brandy or dark rum
- vanilla, cinnamon according to taste
- 2 oz. butter

Directions:
1. Peel and carefully hollow the apples. Prepare stuffing by beating the butter, 3/4 cup of sugar, crushed walnuts, raisins and cinnamon.
2. Fill in the apples with this mixture and situate them in an oiled dish. Sprinkle the apples with 1-2 tbsp. of water and bake in a moderate oven. Serve warm and side it with vanilla ice cream.

Nutrition:
- 107 Calories
- 9g Fats
- 7g Carbohydrates
- 3g Protein

189. Pumpkin Baked with Dry Fruit

Level of difficulty: Novice level
Preparation Time: 10 minutes
Cooking Time: 15 minutes
Servings: 6
Ingredients:
- lb. pumpkin, cut into medium pieces
- 1 cup dry fruit (apricots, plums, apples, raisins)
- 1/2 cup brown sugar

Directions:
1. Soak the dry fruit in some water, drain and discard the water. Cut the pumpkin in medium cubes. At the bottom of a pot arrange a layer of pumpkin pieces, then a layer of dry fruit and then again, some pumpkin. Add a little water.
2. Cover the pot and bring to boil. Simmer until there is no more water. When almost ready add the sugar. Serve warm or cold.

Nutrition:
- 113 Calories
- 8g Fats
- 5g Carbohydrates
- 3g Protein

190. Banana Shake Bowls

Level of difficulty: Novice level
Preparation Time: 5 minutes
Cooking Time: 0 minutes
Servings: 4
Ingredients:
- 4 medium bananas, peeled
- 1 avocado, peeled, pitted and mashed
- ¾ cup almond milk
- ½ teaspoon vanilla extract

Directions:
1. In a blender, meld the bananas with the avocado and the other ingredients, pulse, divide into bowls and store in the fridge until serving.

Nutrition:
- 185 Calories
- 4.3g Fat
- 6g Carbohydrates
- 6.45g Protein

191. Cold Lemon Squares

Level of difficulty: Novice level
Preparation Time: 30 minutes
Cooking Time: 0 minutes
Servings: 4
Ingredients:
- 1 cup avocado oil+ a drizzle
- 2 bananas, peeled and chopped
- 1 tbsp. honey
- ¼ cup lemon juice
- A pinch of lemon zest, grated

Directions:
1. In your food processor, mix the bananas with the rest of the ingredients, pulse well and spread on the bottom of a pan greased with a drizzle of oil. Introduce in the fridge for 30 minutes, slice into squares and serve.

Nutrition:
- 136 Calories
- 11.2g Fat
- 7g Carbohydrates
- 1.1g Protein

192. Blackberry and Apples Cobbler

Level of difficulty: Novice level
Preparation Time: 10 minutes
Cooking Time: 30 minutes
Servings: 6

Ingredients:
- ¾ cup stevia
- 6 cups blackberries
- ¼ cup apples, cored and cubed
- ¼ teaspoon baking powder
- 1 tbsp. lime juice
- ½ cup almond flour
- ½ cup water
- 3 and ½ tbsp. avocado oil
- Cooking spray

Directions:
1. In a bowl, combine the berries with half of the stevia and lemon juice, sprinkle some flour all over, whisk and pour into a baking dish greased with cooking spray.
2. In another bowl, mix flour with the rest of the sugar, baking powder, the water and the oil, and stir the whole thing with your hands. Spread over the berries, introduce in the oven at 375 degrees F and bake for 30 minutes.
3. Serve warm.

Nutrition:
- 221 Calories
- 6.3g Fat
- 6g Carbohydrates
- 9g Protein

193. Black Tea Cake

Level of difficulty: Novice level
Preparation Time: 10 minutes
Cooking Time: 35 minutes
Servings: 8
Ingredients:
- 6 tbsp. black tea powder
- 2 cups almond milk, warmed up
- 1 cup avocado oil
- 2 cups stevia
- 4 eggs
- 2 teaspoons vanilla extract
- 3 and ½ cups almond flour
- 1 teaspoon baking soda
- 3 teaspoons baking powder

Directions:
1. Stir well the almond milk with the oil, stevia and the rest of the ingredients. Pour this into a cake pan lined with parchment paper, introduce in the oven at 350 degrees F and bake for 35 minutes. Leave the cake to cool down, slice and serve.

Nutrition:
- 200 Calories
- 6.4g Fat
- 6.5g Carbohydrates
- 5.4g Protein

194. Green Tea and Vanilla Cream

Level of difficulty: Intermediate
Preparation Time: 2 hours
Cooking Time: 0 minutes
Servings: 4
Ingredients:
- 14 ounces' almond milk, hot
- 2 tbsp. green tea powder
- 14 ounces' heavy cream
- 3 tbsp. stevia
- 1 teaspoon vanilla extract
- 1 teaspoon gelatin powder

Directions:
1. Incorporate well the almond milk with the green tea powder and the rest of the ingredients, cool down, divide into cups and keep in the fridge for 2 hours before serving.

Nutrition:
- 120 Calories
- 3g Fat
- 7g Carbohydrates
- 4g Protein

195. Vermicelli Pudding

Level of difficulty: Novice level
Preparation Time: 10 minutes
Cooking Time: 45 minutes
Servings: 2
Ingredients:
- ½ Cup Vermicelli Noodles
- ½ Cup Sultans
- ½ Teaspoon Vanilla Extract, Pure
- ½ Teaspoon Nutmeg
- 1 Cup Milk
- 2 Tbsp. Sugar
- 2 Eggs

Directions:
1. Start by cooking your vermicelli noodles as your package dictates, and makes sure to drain them.
2. Whisk your eggs, milk and sugar in a bowl.
3. Add in your remaining ingredients.
4. Get out a baking dish and grease it. Place the mixture inside, and then bake at 320 for forty-five minutes.
5. Sprinkle with nutmeg before serving.

Nutrition:
- Calories: 251
- Protein: 11.6 Grams
- Fat: 7.1 Grams
- Carbs: 35.7 Grams
- Sodium: 120 mg

196. Strawberry Compote in Red Wine Syrup

Level of difficulty: Novice level
Preparation Time: 10 minutes
Cooking Time: 20 minutes
Servings: 2
Ingredients:
- 1 cup red wine
- 1/3 Cup granulated sugar
- 1 teaspoon vanilla extract
- ½ teaspoon ground cinnamon
- 4 cups strawberries, hulled and sliced

Directions:
1. In a medium saucepan, bring the wine, sugar, vanilla, and cinnamon to a boil. Reduce heat and simmer until the liquid is reduced by half, about 20 minutes.
2. Place 1 cup of berries into each of 4 cups. Drizzle with 2 tbsp. of the red wine syrup.
3. Serve warm or chill in the refrigerator before serving.

Nutrition:
- Calories: 119
- Total Fat: 0g
- Saturated Fat: 0g
- Protein: 1g
- Carbohydrates: 28g
- Fiber: 3g
- Sodium: 2mg

197. Homemade Caramel-Dipped Apples

Level of difficulty: Novice level
Preparation Time: 10 minutes, plus 15 minutes to chill
Cooking Time: 1 minute
Servings: 2
Ingredients:
- 4 Pink Lady, Honeycrisp, Fuji, or Granny Smith apples
- Cooking spray
- ½ CUP Homemade Caramel Sauce
- ½ cup unsalted peanuts, chopped

Directions:
1. Remove the stems of the apples, and push a wooden skewer into the bottom of each apple, about three quarters of the way through.

2. Line a baking sheet with parchment paper and coat with cooking spray.
3. Warm the caramel sauce in a microwave-safe bowl for 1 minute, stirring frequently.
4. Quickly roll each apple in the caramel sauce. Use a spoon to cover the apple with the sauce.
5. Roll or dip the caramel apples in the chopped nuts, then place on the prepared baking sheet. Refrigerate until the caramel hardens, about 15 minutes.

Nutrition:
- Calories: 311
- Total Fat: 16g
- Saturated Fat: 6g
- Protein: 5g
- Carbohydrates: 40g
- Fiber: 6g
- Sodium: 64mg

198. Pomegranate-Pistachio Bark

Level of difficulty: Novice level
Preparation Time: 10 minutes, plus 45 minutes to chill
Cooking Time: 10 minutes
Servings: 2
Ingredients:
- ½ cup raw shelled pistachios, roughly chopped
- 1 pound 60% dark chocolate, broken into pieces
- ½ cup pomegranate arils, liquid drained
- 1/8 Teaspoon sea salt

Directions:
1. Line a baking sheet with parchment paper. Set aside.
2. Heat a small skillet over medium heat. Add the pistachios and cook until toasted, about 3 minutes. Set aside to cool.
3. In a small saucepan, bring a cup of water to a boil, then reduce heat to a simmer. Place a heat-proof medium bowl on top of the saucepan to make a double boiler. Add the chocolate to the bowl and cook, stirring gently with a wooden spoon until the mixture is smooth, about 5 minutes. Spoon the chocolate onto the prepared baking sheet, spreading to the edges evenly with a spatula.
4. Evenly sprinkle the chocolate with the pistachios, pomegranate arils, and sea salt.
5. Transfer the baking sheet to the refrigerator for about 45 minutes, until the chocolate sets.
6. Break the bark into 24 pieces and serve.

Nutrition:
- Calories: 127
- Total Fat: 8g
- Saturated Fat: 4g
- Protein: 2g
- Carbohydrates: 11g
- Fiber: 2g
- Sodium: 13mg

199. Coconut-Date Pudding

Level of difficulty: Intermediate
Preparation Time: 10 minutes, plus 3 hours to chill
Cooking Time: 10 minutes
Servings: 2
Ingredients:
- 3 cups unsweetened coconut milk, divided
- 1½ cups pitted Medrol dates, chopped
- 4 tbsp. (¼ cup) chopped walnuts
- 3 tbsp. water
- 1 teaspoon gelatin

- 1 teaspoon ground cinnamon

Directions:
1. In a medium saucepan, bring 1 cup of coconut milk and the dates to a boil. Reduce heat to medium-low, and continue cooking, stirring often, until the liquid evaporates, about 5 minutes.
2. Divide the dates between the 4 ramekins, pressing them into the bottom. Top the dates in each ramekin with 1 tbsp. of walnuts.
3. Add the remaining 2 cups of coconut milk to the saucepan, and heat over medium heat.
4. In a small bowl, whisk the water and gelatin, then add to the saucepan. Bring to a boil, reduce heat to medium, and whisk for about 5 minutes, until the gelatin is incorporated. Add the cinnamon, stirring to blend. Remove from heat and allow to slightly cool.
5. Pour the coconut mixture evenly between the 4 ramekins. Loosely cover with plastic wrap, and refrigerate the puddings to set for at least 3 hours or up to overnight.

Nutrition:
- Calories: 334
- Total Fat: 10g
- Saturated Fat: 9g
- Protein: 5g
- Carbohydrates: 67g
- Fiber: 8g
- Sodium: 46mg

200. Honey Almonds

Level of difficulty: Novice level
Preparation Time: 10 minutes
Cooking Time: 0 minutes
Servings: 2

Ingredients:
- 1 Tbsp. Rosemary, Fresh & Minced
- 1 Cup Almonds, Raw & Whole
- 1 Tbsp. Honey, Raw
- ¼ Teaspoon Sea Salt, Fine
- Nonstick Cooking Spray

Directions:
1. Get out a skillet and heat it up over medium heat. In this skillet you'll combine your salt, almonds and rosemary. Mix well. You'll need to cook for a full minute and stir frequently.
2. Drizzle your honey in and cook for another four minutes while stirring frequently. Your almonds should start to darken near the edges and be well coated.
3. Remove your almonds from heat, and spread them onto a pan that's been coated with nonstick cooking spray. They should cool for ten minutes, and then you can break them apart before serving.

Nutrition:
- Calories: 149
- Protein: 5 Grams
- Fat: 12 Grams
- Carbs: 8 Grams
- Sodium: 78 mg

CHAPTER 7. SHOPPING LIST

The Mediterranean diet is superior to other diets because it provides a balance of nutrients and helps prevent chronic disease. The eight-day program has been put together with the intention to educate people on the importance of a healthy lifestyle. Instead of simply adding fruits and vegetables to your daily routine, you have alternatives that will become part of your new lifestyle. It also targets specific lifestyle changes like eating only natural or organic ingredients, fats from olive oil, and lean meat without added salt or sugar. Take note that the food is not for weight loss but to improve your overall health. The main goal is to make it easy to adopt a Mediterranean diet in your daily routine. You will be able to eat a wide variety of food and enjoy them as long as they are prepared using the ingredients from the shopping list.

Non-starchy vegetables (maximum 2-3 servings per day)

Like those found in the Mediterranean diet, these vegetables provide flavor without adding fat or calories. It can be consumed raw, steamed or cooked by boiling. Cooking it with herbs and spices can also add more taste and lower calories. Examples are tomatoes, peppers, mushrooms, eggplant and spinach.

Fruits (maximum 2-3 servings per day)

Foods like fruits and vegetables provide nutrients like vitamins and minerals that are essential in maintaining good health. They can be eaten as is or with the use of fresh juice to avoid calories from sugar. Fresh fruits that you can consume include orange, watermelon, banana, grapes and apple. Mango is an exception because it provides healthy fat in addition to nutrients. It is recommended that you avoid eating canned fruits because it contains added sugar and salt.

Grains (maximum 7 servings per week)

The grains included in the Mediterranean diet should be whole grains without added salt or sugar. They include brown rice, whole wheat bread, bulgur, and whole-grain pasta.

Starchy vegetables (maximum 3 servings per week)

These foods such as corn, potatoes and sweet potatoes are high in carbohydrates and provide energy. They also provide the fiber that can aid digestion in the digestive tract. You should eat these foods raw without adding salt or sugar unless they were prepared with herbs and spices so they do not become too bland. Examples of starchy vegetables are peas, carrots, yams and winter squash.

Grains including bread (maximum 7 servings per week)

Bread is made from grains such as wheat flour or barley flour. Aside from grains, you can also include rice bread, cookies and cakes made using these flours. It is best to avoid eating bread or cakes that have added vegetable oils and refined sugar. These foods are common in most food markets but high in calories and fat.

Dairy (maximum 3 servings per day)

The dairy products that are allowed to be included in the Mediterranean diet include milk, yogurt, cheese and butter made from milk or cream. You should refer to the list of allowed foods so you will know which dairy products are included on a specific day. You should buy whole milk rather than skimmed because it contains more nutrients. This type of dairy also contains less sugar than low-fat varieties. In the Mediterranean diet, yogurts are included because they contain probiotic bacteria that can improve digestive health. You should choose yogurt with live cultures and few ingredients on the label.

Vegetable oils (maximum 7 servings per week)

The vegetable oils included in the diet should have high oleic content. They include virgin olive oil, canola oil, and nut oils. These vegetable oils have omega-9 fatty acid that helps in weight loss as it increases your metabolism and therefore helps you burn more calories.

Nuts (maximum 7 servings per week)

Nuts are high in unsaturated fat and are beneficial for weight loss because they decrease glucose levels after eating a meal during digestion. They also increase your metabolism and therefore help in weight loss.

Beans (maximum 7 servings per week)

Beans are high in fiber. They are also low in saturated fat and high in folate, antioxidants, magnesium, iron, and calcium. Beans contain protein that increases satiety as it improves your health.

Dried fruit (maximum 1 serving per day)

Dried fruits are high in fiber. They also contain monounsaturated fat and therefore can help you lose weight. However, dried fruits have a higher calorie count than fresh fruits so they should be consumed as part of a balanced diet to achieve weight loss goals.

CHAPTER 8. 10 TIPS FOR SUCCESS

Here are some of the easiest ways to make sure you get the most out of your Mediterranean diet, both big and small. These tactics can also assist you in losing weight, if that is one of your goals, by making it easier for you to adapt to and adhere to the diet.

Treat Yourself like A Guest

It's as much about how you eat as it is about what you eat when it comes to the Mediterranean diet. The Mediterranean people have a deep respect for and love for food, which leads them to create beautiful (though often very simple) tables. Bring out the fine china, fill a canning jar with fresh flowers, light some candles, or dine on the patio. Treat every meal as if you were entertaining guests, no matter what.

Learn to Savor

In our fast-paced, multitasking society, we tend to eat without paying attention to the food. We eat while standing up, commuting to work, watching TV, or doing paperwork. This is the polar opposite of Mediterranean custom, where it's not unusual to linger over even a simple meal for several hours, and doing something mundane while eating seems ludicrous.

And if you're eating alone, turn off the television. Put your job, your phone, and all other distractions away. Focus on the wonderful food you're consuming, even though you're getting dinner for one. Taste what's on your plate carefully and begin to enjoy the pleasure of taste.

Become a Social Eater

In the Mediterranean, families, and friends gather around food on a daily basis, even if all that is served is some crusty bread and healthy olive oil. Even simple meals offer an opportunity to invite someone over for some good food and talk. Simple meals are also an opportunity to invite someone over for good food and conversation in the Mediterranean region, where Sunday afternoon dinners are normally an important part of the week. Families will stay at the table even though there are no visitors to chat about the day and enjoy each other's company.

Inviting friends and family to a casual summer lunch or a casual dinner party is a perfect way to bring the Mediterranean way of eating into your own life. Eating is as much about the business as it is about the food for Mediterranean people, and meals do taste better when shared.

Learn to Make Substitutions

The Mediterranean diet permits the consumption of a wide variety of foods, but balance is important. Learn to make substitutions if you're missing something you shouldn't be eating, such as greasy French fries or crispy potato chips. It's possible that the substitute for your favorite junk food will become your new favorite!

Kale chips are more flavorful than store-bought potato chips, and they're free of unhealthy fats, salt, and preservatives. A refreshing homemade granita takes no time to prepare, has unrivaled flavor, and is much healthier than the ice cream you're used to.

Get Some Moderate Exercise Every Day—Preferably Outdoors

In the Mediterranean, spending time outdoors is a normal part of life. The region is blessed with sunshine and pleasant weather, as well as stunning scenery and warm oceans. If they're working in the garden, walking on the beach, or tossing a ball for the dog, people spend as much time outdoors as they do inside.

Three days a week, try to get at least thirty minutes of moderate exercise. This has been shown to be a significant component of weight loss, cardiovascular health improvement, and general satisfaction and well-being.

Try going for a walk in the morning or after work, enrolling in a ballroom dancing class, swimming in a pool or the beach, playing catch with the kids, or engaging in some other activity that gets you moving. It doesn't have to be strenuous, and it shouldn't be the same thing every day.

Don't Tempt Yourself

Don't hold pastries in the pantry or chicken nuggets in the fridge only because they haven't expired. Having foods at home that aren't on your diet or that you appear to overeat is tantamount to tempting fate. If you're looking for something to serve guests, the Mediterranean menu has a lot of options. There are no situations under which you would need chicken nuggets. Give them to the family next door!

Don't Overwhelm Yourself

Avoid making your life more difficult by planning three weeks' worth of meals ahead of time or trying ten new recipes in a week.

Take things slowly and cultivate a laid-back attitude toward your new eating habits. Try a few new recipes, but don't make them all complicated dishes that will just add to your stress level.

The majority of Mediterranean dishes are basic, requiring few ingredients and easy preparation. To prepare delicious meals, you don't need to take a lot of fancy moves.

Give Yourself a Break

So you went to a fast-food joint and ordered the messiest, most calorie-dense burger they had. Hopefully, it was absolutely delectable. Now is the time to move on. One blunder isn't going to ruin you. Don't eat garbage for three days because you're mad about a blunder!

Try Something New Each Week

Eating the Mediterranean way should be fun, exciting, and even a little exotic. Try to choose one unfamiliar fruit, vegetable, fish, or another ingredient each week. It'll keep things interesting and enhance that sense of voyaging to another land.

Try Growing Your Own

The people of the Mediterranean region are very garden-focused. It's common for them to have lush kitchen gardens in their backyards, and even many city dwellers insist on a few pots of fresh herbs on the windowsill. Growing your herbs and vegetables is fun, saves money, and is the best way to taste something at its very freshest.

CHAPTER 9. 12-WEEK MEAL PROGRAM

Week 1

Days	Breakfast	Lunch	Dinner	Snack/Dessert
1	Secret Breakfast Sundaes	Beef Kofta	Savoy Cabbage with Coconut Cream Sauce	Chocolate Matcha Balls
2	Greek Yogurt Pancakes	Herb Roasted Lamb Chops	Slow-Cooked Buttery Mushrooms	Chia Almond Butter Pudding
3	Greek Yogurt w/Berries & Seeds	Grilled Salmon with Lemon and Wine	Steamed Squash Chowder	Refreshing Strawberry Popsicles
4	Mediterranean Breakfast Egg White Sandwich	Beer-batter Fish	Steamed Zucchini-Paprika	Dark Chocolate Mousse
5	Breakfast Taco Scramble	Pickled Apple	Stir-Fried Brussels sprouts and Carrots	Warm & Soft Baked Pears
6	Blueberry Greek Yogurt Pancakes	Baked Clams Oreganata	Stir-Fried Eggplant	Healthy & Quick Energy Bites
7	Cauliflower Fritters with Hummus	Tuna Tartare	Summer Vegetables	Creamy Yogurt Banana Bowls

Week 2

Days	Breakfast	Lunch	Dinner	Snack/Dessert
1	Secret Breakfast Sundaes	Beef Kofta	Savoy Cabbage with Coconut Cream Sauce	Chocolate Matcha Balls
2	Greek Yogurt Pancakes	Herb Roasted Lamb Chops	Slow-Cooked Buttery Mushrooms	Chia Almond Butter Pudding
3	Greek Yogurt w/Berries & Seeds	Grilled Salmon with Lemon and Wine	Steamed Squash Chowder	Refreshing Strawberry Popsicles
4	Mediterranean Breakfast Egg White Sandwich	Beer-batter Fish	Steamed Zucchini-Paprika	Dark Chocolate Mousse
5	Breakfast Taco Scramble	Pickled Apple	Stir-Fried Brussels sprouts and Carrots	Warm & Soft Baked Pears
6	Blueberry Greek Yogurt Pancakes	Baked Clams Oreganata	Stir-Fried Eggplant	Healthy & Quick Energy Bites
7	Cauliflower Fritters with Hummus	Tuna Tartare	Summer Vegetables	Creamy Yogurt Banana Bowls

Week 3

Days	Breakfast	Lunch	Dinner	Snack/Dessert
1	Secret Breakfast Sundaes	Beef Kofta	Savoy Cabbage with Coconut Cream Sauce	Chocolate Matcha Balls
2	Greek Yogurt Pancakes	Herb Roasted Lamb Chops	Slow-Cooked Buttery Mushrooms	Chia Almond Butter Pudding
3	Greek Yogurt w/Berries & Seeds	Grilled Salmon with Lemon and Wine	Steamed Squash Chowder	Refreshing Strawberry Popsicles
4	Mediterranean Breakfast Egg White Sandwich	Beer-batter Fish	Steamed Zucchini-Paprika	Dark Chocolate Mousse
5	Breakfast Taco Scramble	Pickled Apple	Stir-Fried Brussels sprouts and Carrots	Warm & Soft Baked Pears
6	Blueberry Greek Yogurt Pancakes	Baked Clams Oreganata	Stir-Fried Eggplant	Healthy & Quick Energy Bites
7	Cauliflower Fritters with Hummus	Tuna Tartare	Summer Vegetables	Creamy Yogurt Banana Bowls

Week 4

Days	Breakfast	Lunch	Dinner	Snack/Dessert
1	Secret Breakfast Sundaes	Beef Kofta	Savoy Cabbage with Coconut Cream Sauce	Chocolate Matcha Balls
2	Greek Yogurt Pancakes	Herb Roasted Lamb Chops	Slow-Cooked Buttery Mushrooms	Chia Almond Butter Pudding
3	Greek Yogurt w/Berries & Seeds	Grilled Salmon with Lemon and Wine	Steamed Squash Chowder	Refreshing Strawberry Popsicles
4	Mediterranean Breakfast Egg White Sandwich	Beer-batter Fish	Steamed Zucchini-Paprika	Dark Chocolate Mousse
5	Breakfast Taco Scramble	Pickled Apple	Stir-Fried Brussels sprouts and Carrots	Warm & Soft Baked Pears
6	Blueberry Greek Yogurt Pancakes	Baked Clams Oreganata	Stir-Fried Eggplant	Healthy & Quick Energy Bites
7	Cauliflower Fritters with Hummus	Tuna Tartare	Summer Vegetables	Creamy Yogurt Banana Bowls

Week 5

Days	Breakfast	Lunch	Dinner	Snack/Dessert
1	Secret Breakfast Sundaes	Beef Kofta	Savoy Cabbage with Coconut Cream Sauce	Chocolate Matcha Balls
2	Greek Yogurt Pancakes	Herb Roasted Lamb Chops	Slow-Cooked Buttery Mushrooms	Chia Almond Butter Pudding
3	Greek Yogurt w/Berries & Seeds	Grilled Salmon with Lemon and Wine	Steamed Squash Chowder	Refreshing Strawberry Popsicles
4	Mediterranean Breakfast Egg White Sandwich	Beer-batter Fish	Steamed Zucchini-Paprika	Dark Chocolate Mousse
5	Breakfast Taco Scramble	Pickled Apple	Stir-Fried Brussels sprouts and Carrots	Warm & Soft Baked Pears
6	Blueberry Greek Yogurt Pancakes	Baked Clams Oreganata	Stir-Fried Eggplant	Healthy & Quick Energy Bites
7	Cauliflower Fritters with Hummus	Tuna Tartare	Summer Vegetables	Creamy Yogurt Banana Bowls

Week 6

Days	Breakfast	Lunch	Dinner	Snack/Dessert
1	Greek Yogurt Pancakes	Beef Kofta	Slow-Cooked Buttery Mushrooms	Chocolate Matcha Balls
2	Greek Yogurt w/Berries & Seeds	Herb Roasted Lamb Chops	Steamed Squash Chowder	Chia Almond Butter Pudding
3	Mediterranean Breakfast Egg White Sandwich	Grilled Salmon with Lemon and Wine	Steamed Zucchini-Paprika	Refreshing Strawberry Popsicles
4	Breakfast Taco Scramble	Beer-batter Fish	Stir-Fried Brussels sprouts and Carrots	Dark Chocolate Mousse
5	Cauliflower Fritters with Hummus	Sole with Spinach	Stir-Fried Eggplant	Warm & Soft Baked Pears
6	Feta and Quinoa Egg Muffins	Pickled Apple	Summer Vegetables	Healthy & Quick Energy Bites
7	5-Minute Heirloom Tomato and Cucumber Toast	Baked Clams Oreganata	Stir-Fried Bok Choy	Creamy Yogurt Banana Bowls

Week 7

Days	Breakfast	Lunch	Dinner	Snack/Dessert
1	Greek Yogurt Pancakes	Beef Kofta	Slow-Cooked Buttery Mushrooms	Chocolate Matcha Balls
2	Greek Yogurt w/Berries & Seeds	Herb Roasted Lamb Chops	Steamed Squash Chowder	Chia Almond Butter Pudding
3	Mediterranean Breakfast Egg White Sandwich	Grilled Salmon with Lemon and Wine	Steamed Zucchini-Paprika	Refreshing Strawberry Popsicles
4	Breakfast Taco Scramble	Beer-batter Fish	Stir-Fried Brussels sprouts and Carrots	Dark Chocolate Mousse
5	Cauliflower Fritters with Hummus	Sole with Spinach	Stir-Fried Eggplant	Warm & Soft Baked Pears
6	Feta and Quinoa Egg Muffins	Pickled Apple	Summer Vegetables	Healthy & Quick Energy Bites
7	5-Minute Heirloom Tomato and Cucumber Toast	Baked Clams Oreganata	Stir-Fried Bok Choy	Creamy Yogurt Banana Bowls

Week 8

Days	Breakfast	Lunch	Dinner	Snack/Dessert
1	Greek Yogurt Pancakes	Beef Kofta	Slow-Cooked Buttery Mushrooms	Chocolate Matcha Balls
2	Greek Yogurt w/Berries & Seeds	Herb Roasted Lamb Chops	Steamed Squash Chowder	Chia Almond Butter Pudding
3	Mediterranean Breakfast Egg White Sandwich	Grilled Salmon with Lemon and Wine	Steamed Zucchini-Paprika	Refreshing Strawberry Popsicles
4	Breakfast Taco Scramble	Beer-batter Fish	Stir-Fried Brussels sprouts and Carrots	Dark Chocolate Mousse
5	Cauliflower Fritters with Hummus	Sole with Spinach	Stir-Fried Eggplant	Warm & Soft Baked Pears
6	Feta and Quinoa Egg Muffins	Pickled Apple	Summer Vegetables	Healthy & Quick Energy Bites
7	5-Minute Heirloom Tomato and Cucumber Toast	Baked Clams Oreganata	Stir-Fried Bok Choy	Creamy Yogurt Banana Bowls

Week 9

Days	Breakfast	Lunch	Dinner	Snack/Dessert
1	Greek Yogurt Pancakes	Beef Kofta	Slow-Cooked Buttery Mushrooms	Chocolate Matcha Balls
2	Greek Yogurt w/Berries & Seeds	Herb Roasted Lamb Chops	Steamed Squash Chowder	Chia Almond Butter Pudding
3	Mediterranean Breakfast Egg White Sandwich	Grilled Salmon with Lemon and Wine	Steamed Zucchini-Paprika	Refreshing Strawberry Popsicles
4	Breakfast Taco Scramble	Beer-batter Fish	Stir-Fried Brussels sprouts and Carrots	Dark Chocolate Mousse
5	Cauliflower Fritters with Hummus	Sole with Spinach	Stir-Fried Eggplant	Warm & Soft Baked Pears
6	Feta and Quinoa Egg Muffins	Pickled Apple	Summer Vegetables	Healthy & Quick Energy Bites
7	5-Minute Heirloom Tomato and Cucumber Toast	Baked Clams Oreganata	Stir-Fried Bok Choy	Creamy Yogurt Banana Bowls

Week 10

Days	Breakfast	Lunch	Dinner	Snack/Dessert
1	Greek Yogurt Pancakes	Beef Kofta	Slow-Cooked Buttery Mushrooms	Chocolate Matcha Balls
2	Greek Yogurt w/Berries & Seeds	Herb Roasted Lamb Chops	Steamed Squash Chowder	Chia Almond Butter Pudding
3	Mediterranean Breakfast Egg White Sandwich	Grilled Salmon with Lemon and Wine	Steamed Zucchini-Paprika	Refreshing Strawberry Popsicles
4	Breakfast Taco Scramble	Beer-batter Fish	Stir-Fried Brussels sprouts and Carrots	Dark Chocolate Mousse
5	Cauliflower Fritters with Hummus	Sole with Spinach	Stir-Fried Eggplant	Warm & Soft Baked Pears
6	Feta and Quinoa Egg Muffins	Pickled Apple	Summer Vegetables	Healthy & Quick Energy Bites
7	5-Minute Heirloom Tomato and Cucumber Toast	Baked Clams Oreganata	Stir-Fried Bok Choy	Creamy Yogurt Banana Bowls

Week 11

Days	Breakfast	Lunch	Dinner	Snack/Dessert
1	Greek Yogurt Pancakes	Herb Roasted Lamb Chops	Stir-Fried Eggplant	Chocolate Matcha Balls
2	Blueberry Greek Yogurt Pancakes	Beer-batter Fish	Summer Veggies in Instant Pot	Chia Almond Butter Pudding
3	Feta Frittata	Pickled Apple	Berries and Grilled Calamari	Refreshing Strawberry Popsicles
4	Roasted Eggplant Salad	Cod Cakes	Crazy Saganaki Shrimp	Dark Chocolate Mousse
5	Mediterranean Eggs Cups	Burrata Caprese Stack	Cucumber-Basil Salsa on Halibut Pouches	Warm & Soft Baked Pears
6	Mediterranean Feta and Quinoa Egg Muffins	Salmon-Stuffed Cucumbers	Grilled Chicken and Zucchini Kebabs	Healthy & Quick Energy Bites
7	Date and Walnut Overnight Oats	Greek Eggplant Dip	Gyro Burgers with Tahini Sauce	Creamy Yogurt Banana Bowls

Week 12

Days	Breakfast	Lunch	Dinner	Snack/Dessert
1	Greek Yogurt Pancakes	Herb Roasted Lamb Chops	Stir-Fried Eggplant	Refreshing Strawberry Popsicles
2	Blueberry Greek Yogurt Pancakes	Beer-batter Fish	Summer Veggies in Instant Pot	Roasted Parmesan Broccoli
3	Feta Frittata	Pickled Apple	Berries and Grilled Calamari	Hummus with Ground Lamb
4	Roasted Eggplant Salad	Cod Cakes	Crazy Saganaki Shrimp	Avocado Dip
5	Mediterranean Eggs Cups	Burrata Caprese Stack	Cucumber-Basil Salsa on Halibut Pouches	Easy roasted fruit recipe
6	Mediterranean Feta and Quinoa Egg Muffins	Salmon-Stuffed Cucumbers	Grilled Chicken and Zucchini Kebabs	Fruit Compote
7	Date and Walnut Overnight Oats	Greek Eggplant Dip	Gyro Burgers with Tahini Sauce	Brown Betty Apple Dessert

CONCLUSION

The Mediterranean diet focuses on whole food ingredients, instead of highly processed meal options. This cookbook is a way for you to try your hand at living healthier while still indulging in some of your favorite Mediterranean foods with this easy-to-follow guide!

This book will help you understand how to plan for meals and snacks during the day. It comes as no surprise that carb intake is not allowed, but sticking with low or non-existent amounts of carbs will yield an amazing wide range of benefits for your body.

Sometimes it can be a challenge to make the right choices about your food. You decide you want a salad, but then you realize the vinaigrette contained sugar or corn syrup, and therefore the benefits of eating that salad are far outweighed by what you are consuming.

The book also contains easy to follow recipes for common Mediterranean foods:

You will still be able to enjoy some of your favorite meals, with a little change here and there. This cookbook takes out the guesswork in making sure that what is in your food is beneficial for health. No more high-fat cheeses to clog your arteries or high carb desserts that will make you gain weight.

You can lower your blood pressure, lose fat and gain muscle with a meal plan that works well for your body! Make smart choices about what you are eating and see the amazing results that come as a result.

Made in the USA
Monee, IL
23 November 2021